OVERCOMI

WINDY DRYDEN was bor
worked in psychotherapy and
years, and is the author or
including *The Incredible Sulk* and
Ten Steps to Positive Living (Sheldon Press, 1994). Dr
Dryden is Professor of Counselling at Goldsmiths College,
University of London.

Overcoming Common Problems Series

For a full list of titles please contact
Sheldon Press, Marylebone Road, London NW1 4DU

Overcoming Common Problems Series

Overcoming Common Problems Series

Overcoming Common Problems

OVERCOMING SHAME

Dr Windy Dryden

sheldon PRESS

First published in Great Britain in 1997 by
Sheldon Press, SPCK, Marylebone Road, London NW1 4DU

© Dr Windy Dryden 1997

British Library Cataloguing-in-Publication Data
A catalogue record for this book is available from the British Library

ISBN 0–85969–718–5

Photoset by Deltatype Ltd, Birkenhead, Merseyside
Printed in Great Britain by
Biddles Ltd, Guildford and King's Lynn

Contents

I dedicate this book to Dr Paul Hauck, whose self-help books have inspired me to write my own.

1

The people behind the feeling

This is a book about shame and how to overcome it. In it I will
outline my view of the important factors that need to be considered
when arriving at a full understanding of this complex emotion. If
you have read my other books for Sheldon Press, it will come as no
surprise for you to learn that my ideas are heavily influenced by the
pioneering work of an American clinical psychologist named
Albert Ellis. Dr Ellis originated an approach to counselling and
psychotherapy that I practise called Rational Emotive Behaviour
Therapy (REBT). I will outline the basics of REBT as it pertains to
shame in Chapter 3.

However, before I begin to discuss shame, I want to present some
brief case histories to show the people behind the feeling of shame
and to illustrate that shame can be about a variety of issues. Please
note that I will return to some of these case histories throughout the
book to help the ideas that I will present here come alive, as it were.
You will meet them all again in the final chapter where I will discuss
how they did or could overcome their shame problem.

Marie

Marie had worked for seven months as a personal assistant to a
high-flying executive with whom she had a good relationship.
She realized that he had high standards for his employees and she
respected him for this. In his dealings with Marie, her boss was
very fair. If she made a mistake he would correct her, but in a way
that Marie could learn from. He focused on her error without
criticizing her as a person. He was also quick to offer praise for a
job well done.

Marie's boss was, in general, professional in his dealings with
her and with his other staff. He was polite and never seemed to
bring any problems that he had in his personal life into the office.
One day, however, Marie noticed that her boss seemed quite

gruff with her. He seemed to find fault with everything she did. Even the coffee that she made for him wasn't the right strength. Marie could feel herself becoming quite upset as the day wore on, as she disliked bad feelings between people.

At the end of this particular day, Marie's boss called her into his office and pointed out some basic typing mistakes she had made which were probably due to the increased tension she felt during the day. This time her boss was not fair and measured in his criticism. He raised his voice with Marie (something he had never done before) and told her in no uncertain terms that she wasn't worth the money he was paying her. At this point Marie could contain her feelings no longer and she burst into tears. As soon as she realized that she had started crying, Marie experienced strong feelings of shame about her behaviour which she inferred demonstrated that she had publicly revealed a weakness. She could not look her boss in the eye and felt an overwhelming impulse to run out of the room which, in fact, she did.

As soon as she got home, Marie reviewed this incident in her mind. She focused on the fact that she had cried in front of her boss, inferred that this was a dreadful weakness and felt ashamed all over again. In her state of shame, Marie began to think that her boss would look down on her for crying, that he would tell everyone in the office who would then either look down on her or pity her. She thought that everyone would hear about this incident and would remember it forever. She resolved there and then to avoid her boss as much as possible and certainly when she was upset, and decided from that moment to keep herself to herself when it came to dealing with her work colleagues.

Elise

Elise was a young Orthodox Jewish woman who had grown up without any sexual education. She recognized at quite an early age that she had strong sexual feelings, but she had no outlet to express them. One night she had an erotic dream where she was caressing and being caressed by another woman. She felt deeply ashamed about this and about the fact that she experienced an orgasm during this dream. Knowing very little about female sexuality and feeling deeply ashamed about the sexual feelings that she experienced during the dream, Elise concluded that she must be a lesbian, a realization that she found horrific. She then tried to avoid looking at women and tried to keep her physical distance from them. This only made things worse and she found herself unwittingly looking at the breasts and crotches of other women in the street.

On realizing that she was becoming more and more aware of other women as sexual beings, she became increasingly ashamed and resolved to avoid all situations where women might be. Since she was a college student and had to study with other women, her increasing feelings of shame led her to think that her fellow students (especially the female students) would know that she was a lesbian, that people in her religious community would find out and that she would become an outcast. She came to see me for counselling specifically because I was a man. Furthermore, she was convinced that she would never marry and have children and when I first saw her she was quite suicidal.

Rick

Rick was a leading member of a local street gang whose code of honour was that whatever happened gang members stuck together and would never betray another gang member. One day Rick's gang got into a fight with another gang which got more violent than the previous clashes between the two gangs. During this fight one of the members of the other gang was stabbed and needed intensive care at the local hospital. The police made their enquiries and arrested Rick, Steve and Geoff (two other gang members). Rick and Steve resisted all attempts from the police to tell them who had stabbed the member from the other gang even though they knew very well who was the guilty party.

Geoff, on the other hand, 'grassed' and told the police that Freddy was the gang member who had stabbed the unfortunate member of the other gang. When it became known what Geoff had done, virtually all the gang members were furious with Geoff

3

and resolved to exact retribution from him. Rick, however, was more ashamed than angry. He was ashamed about Geoff's behaviour because Geoff had broken the gang's code of honour and according to Rick had shown the gang in a very bad light in the local community. Rick's feelings of shame led him to keep a very low profile in the community, avoiding all places where members of other gangs might be found. His shame also led him to think that as a result of Geoff's behaviour other people in the community would hold Rick and his gang in contempt in that they had 'gone soft' and were no longer a force to be reckoned with in 'gangland'.

Tom

Tom was a good-looking young man in his early twenties. However, he was 5'2" in height and deeply ashamed of this. In his heart of hearts he considered himself to be a wimp, someone whom other men would laugh at and women would feel sorry for. To make up for his lack of height, Tom would seize on every opportunity to show other people (and, of course, himself) how macho he was. To help him do this he studied martial arts and pumped iron. He would deliberately pick fights with taller guys, taking great satisfaction in beating them up. He would revel in picking up and seducing women taller than himself. 'Love 'em and leave 'em' was Tom's motto.

However, one day he picked on the wrong guy. Unbeknown to him, Tom's adversary, a 6'1" man, had a black belt in karate and thrashed Tom in the ensuing fight. Tom fought with all his might, but Lee, his opponent, was too strong and too skilful for Tom who ended up with several cuts and bruises. Tom felt deeply ashamed of the beating he took at the hands of Lee and resolved there and then to move as far as he could away from the neighbourhood where his terrible beating took place. This is exactly what Tom did. He moved to a different part of the country and resolved never to return to his home town since he was convinced that people would still remember the day when he was revealed in his true colours as a 'weak wimp'.

4

Bernice

Bernice was a woman in her mid-thirties who was divorced with two children. Bernice had been sexually abused by an uncle when she was eight and, as is quite common in such cases, she kept this information to herself. She had the sense then that what her uncle did to her was wrong and dirty and she considered that if she told her parents they would not believe her. The legacy that she was left with was shame. Bernice was ashamed that she let her uncle abuse her without putting up a struggle and she was ashamed about her body, believing even in adulthood that her body would reveal her shameful secret.

Because of her feelings of shame, Bernice had sexual problems which led in part to the break-up of her marriage. She could only have intercourse if she was drunk, and refused to let anyone see her naked body lest they would learn her secret. She generally avoided any kind of sexual contact if she could, because it reminded her of what her uncle did to her. Once her feelings of shame were activated, Bernice thought that if others saw any part of her body (i) they would see her as a shameful person for having let her uncle abuse her; (ii) they would consider her a sexually promiscuous woman who was 'asking for it'; and (iii) they would be revolted by her body. Thus, when she felt ashamed, she would cover herself from head to toe even on hot summer days to hide her mark of shame.

Mohammed

Mohammed was a young man in his mid-twenties who came from a very traditional Muslim family and lived with them in a close-knit Muslim community. Both his family and this close community strongly emphasized the importance of upstanding behaviour on the part of its members in the wider context of British society.

Mohammed was in many respects a good Muslim, but he had a low tolerance for frustration and was also impulsive. This meant that whenever he saw something that he really wanted, he would somehow find the money to buy it as soon as possible. He just

5

couldn't wait. Unfortunately, this meant that at times Mohammed would break the law in order to obtain the financial wherewithal to fund his spending habit. He would steal mainly credit cards and use them, having developed the skill to forge other people's signatures.

For a time Mohammed was fortunate and he got away with breaking the law. This, however, led him to think that he had a good system and wouldn't get caught. This overconfidence was Mohammed's undoing in that he took one risk too many and was arrested for credit-card fraud. In the event, and after a period on remand, Mohammed was found guilty, but as it was his first criminal offence and he had spent six months on remand, he received a short jail sentence.

You can imagine from what I have said what impact all this had on Mohammed's family and local community. Initially, everybody was shocked and devastated. In prison Mohammed felt deep and intense shame for his actions and for showing his family, community and religion in a very bad light. As a result of his feelings of shame, Mohammed refused to see any visitors and gave up following the Muslim faith. He thought that on release he would be treated as a pariah by his family and community and that no one who knew him would ever forget what he had done. He also had visions of young children pointing him out in the street as some kind of leper.

Sarah

Sarah was a 33-year-old woman who suffered from chronic feelings of general shame. This meant that she felt ashamed much of the time and had done so for many years. For as long as she could remember, Sarah viewed herself as a defective person whom others would find repellent if they got to know her. Sarah held this belief very strongly and it seemed that nothing could shake it. Not only did this belief lead to Sarah feeling shame a lot in her life in a broad range of situations where she considered she had to be present; it also meant that Sarah avoided many social situations at which she would like to be present but where her presence was optional.

You might suppose that Sarah had had a very bad childhood, but this was not the case. She was very much loved by her parents and by her elder brother. She did have difficulty making friends at school and joining in with other kids there and this led her to withdraw into herself and to escape into her own private fantasy world. The other kids at school left Sarah alone and neither bullied her nor ridiculed her. Yet from her early schoolgirl experiences Sarah developed the idea that she was defective and that others would not want to know her if they found out what she really was like. So into adolescence and early adulthood, Sarah avoided others and kept herself to herself. Because of this avoidance, Sarah failed to acquire the social skills that would enable her, at the very least, to get by socially. Because she lacked these social skills, Sarah was constantly saying inappropriate things in public. She quickly felt ashamed as soon as she became aware of what she had said, which she saw as further evidence that she was defective.

You have now met Marie, Elise, Rick, Tom, Bernice, Mohammed and Sarah. You will meet some of them in the following chapters where I will use their stories to illustrate some of the important factors that you need to consider if you are to understand the emotion of shame. In addition, you will meet them all again in the final chapter where I will show how they all did or could overcome their feelings of shame.

2

What people feel ashamed about

In this chapter, I will consider what we feel ashamed about when we experience this emotion. Before I do so, I want to discuss briefly the difference between actual events and inferences. It is important that you grasp the difference between these two things if you are to understand fully what we feel ashamed about as human beings.

Actual events and inferences

Briefly, as its name suggests, an actual event is something that you can prove actually happened. It accurately represents reality. An inference, on the other hand, is an attempt to describe accurately what happened but it needs to be tested against reality to see if it is true or false. An inference may be true and if so, it attains the status of an actual event, but without checking your inference against reality you cannot regard it as an actual event.

Let me illustrate the above point. Let's suppose that I am giving a lecture and you are in the audience. I suddenly stop talking and stand with my back to you, facing a window with my head slightly inclined. Now, if I asked you to describe exactly what I was doing, what would you say? I have carried out this exercise many times when giving lectures on psychological topics and the chances are that you would give the same answer that most people give. They reply: 'You are looking out of the window.' Now, is this an actual event or an inference? The correct answer is that it is an inference. You don't know for sure whether or not I have my eyes open. In fact, for the purposes of this exercise I always stand facing the window with my eyes closed to demonstrate that the statement 'You are looking out of the window' is not an actual event, but an inference which when tested in this case is not factual.

Shame-related inferences

When you feel shame it is usually because you make a number of inferences which may or may not be correct. These inferences are what you are ashamed about. Let's go back to the case material presented in Chapter 1, to see what inferences some of the people made.

(1) Marie felt ashamed about crying in front of her boss because she considered that she had publicly revealed a weakness.

(2) Elise felt ashamed about her sexual feelings because she inferred that she was a lesbian.

(3) Rick felt ashamed when Geoff 'grassed' to the police because he considered that Geoff broke the gang's code of honour and showed the gang in a bad light in the local community. Remember that Rick closely identified with his gang.

(4) Tom felt ashamed about his inference that being beaten up revealed him as a wimp in the eyes of those who witnessed the beating and of those who might learn about it in the future.

(5) Bernice felt ashamed about her body because she inferred that it revealed that she had been sexually abused and as a result others would conclude that she was a shameful person and treat her accordingly.

These examples illustrate common issues about which people feel ashamed. Before I discuss these issues more generally, it is worth remembering that when you feel the emotion of shame you do not tend to distinguish between actual events and inferences. To you, your inferences are actual events, full stop. Thus, in the fourth example above, Tom does not consider his inference that he will be viewed by others as a wimp as anything other than a fact.

What are the common issues that you feel ashamed about? Let me now outline them in general terms.

Falling short (and often very short) of your ideal

You tend to feel ashamed when you fall short of your ideal, particularly when this occurs in a social context or is related to some kind of social code. The word 'social' is important here in that shame is very much a 'social' emotion. As I will discuss presently, shame occurs either when others are present or when the presence of others is in the forefront of your mind when you are alone reflecting on something you have done, for example.

It was once thought that people feel ashamed about any kind of failure to achieve their ideal, and certainly some people do feel ashamed when they fall *just* short of their ideal. However, recent research has shown that you feel ashamed most often when you fall *very* short of your ideal. One psychologist put this very well by saying that you feel ashamed about achieving your anti-ideal i.e. when you behave, for example, in a way that is the very opposite or approaching the very opposite of your ideal.

Let me illustrate the difference between falling just short of your ideal and achieving your anti-ideal by assuming that you consider that acting politely towards people constitutes your ideal. You may fall just short of your ideal by failing to use someone's proper title or you may achieve your anti-ideal if you insult someone's good name in front of them and in the presence of other people. You may feel ashamed in both of these instances, but as I have just pointed out, recent psychological research has shown that you are more likely to feel ashamed in the latter example than in the former.

To which types of events am I referring here? Here is a list of events (actual or inferred) about which you tend to feel ashamed.

(1) Behaviour

First, under this heading, you can feel ashamed about what you do. Examples are:

(i) You infer that you have revealed a weakness (e.g. Marie felt ashamed when she cried in front of her boss).

(ii) You infer that you have acted in a way that breaks an important social code (e.g. you remain seated when the national anthem is played at a public gathering).

Second, under this heading, you can feel ashamed about what you failed to do. Examples are:

(i) You have failed to act honourably (e.g. you infer that you have failed to go to the aid of someone who needs help).

(ii) You infer that you have failed to act in a way that observes an important social convention (e.g. you inadvertently do not wear appropriate attire at a formal event).

(2) Thoughts and images

Under this heading, you feel ashamed about finding yourself thinking thoughts or having images which you deem to be forbidden, but which do not necessarily relate to your moral code (e.g. Elise having thoughts which she infers means that she is a lesbian).

(3) Emotions

Here you feel ashamed about experiencing an emotion that you consider to be an anti-ideal. Thus, you may have as your ideal feeling loving kindness for your enemies, whereas in reality you feel murderous towards them. Your murderous rage constitutes your anti-ideal about which you feel ashamed. Incidentally, you can feel ashamed about your feelings of shame if you regard them to be a weakness.

(4) Bodily blemishes and deformities

Here you consider that part of your body is blemished or deformed in some way and this blemish or deformity (e.g. a visible scar, a very long nose or a small penis) is something that constitutes an anti-ideal. In a psychiatric condition known as body dysmorphic disorder (BDD), the sufferer is deeply ashamed of an aspect of his or her body which she regards as a defect, but others in reality consider within normal limits. This example stresses the importance of considering the person's inferences about their body rather than the 'facts' of their situation.

Letting down your reference group

The second category of events about which you tend to feel ashamed that I wish to discuss concerns your inferences that you have let down your reference group and shown that group in a bad

11

light. In modern parlance, you have brought your reference group 'into disrepute'. A reference group, by the way, is any grouping of people with whom you closely identify. An example of this category is provided by the case example of Mohammed discussed in Chapter 1. Mohammed, you will recall, felt ashamed primarily about letting down his family, local community and religious reference groups by his criminal actions.

Being let down by a member of your reference group

The third category of events that you may feel ashamed about concerns not your own behaviour, but the behaviour of a member (or members) of your reference group. An example of this category is represented by the case of Rick (see Chapter 1). Rick, you will recall, felt ashamed when Geoff, a member of his gang, 'grassed' to the police. Rick was ashamed about Geoff's behaviour because he inferred that Geoff (i) broke the gang's code of honour; and (ii) showed his gang in a bad light in the local community. Rick again closely identified with his reference group (i.e. his gang).

Being a reflection of how others treat you and/or think about you when you haven't done anything to merit such behaviour and/or attitude

In this category you tend to feel ashamed about the way others treat you and/or think of you when you haven't done anything to merit their behaviour and/or attitude. You think that their behaviour and attitude constitute an invitation for you to evaluate yourself in a certain way. As we will see in Chapter 3, you respond to this invitation by evaluating yourself in a way that leads you to feel ashamed. An example of this is found in the case of Bernice (see Chapter 1) who felt ashamed about being sexually abused by her uncle even though she hadn't done anything to warrant her feelings of shame. She viewed this act as a stimulus to self-evaluation.

Indeed, you may feel ashamed when you have actually acted in an honourable manner as long as someone thinks that you haven't and disapproves of you. I remember feeling ashamed as a young man when I intervened to help a friend who was in danger of being attacked, when other people present thought my intervention was unwarranted and disapproved of me for my behaviour.

Being exposed to the judgement of others

I mentioned earlier that shame is a social emotion. This means that you tend to feel ashamed when you are in the actual presence of other people or when you think of the responses of others when you are alone. While you mostly feel shame when other people are present to witness your 'shameful' behaviour, for example, the actual presence of others is not a necessary condition for the experience of shame. You can and do feel ashamed when you are on your own, thinking about the way you have acted. When you do this, however, you do have other people in mind. Thus, others do need to be present psychologically rather than physically for you to experience shame when you have acted 'shamefully'.

When you feel ashamed, you infer that others who may be actually or psychologically present are judging you in some negative way. More specifically, you infer that they either look down on you or will shun you in some way. For example, Tom (see Chapter 1) thought that others would discover that he had been beaten up and that they would look down on him (think of him as a wimp).

Summary

In this chapter, I have discussed what people tend to feel ashamed about. I have pointed out that you tend to feel ashamed (i) when you fall short and most often very short of your ideal; (ii) when you let down your reference group; (iii) when you are let down by a member of your reference group; (iv) when others treat you or think of you as meriting shame when in fact you do not; and (v) when others look down on you or shun you in your mind or in reality. I have also stressed that you feel ashamed about such matters whether they are actual or inferred events. The important point is that you consider them to be actual events.

However, while these constitute events about which you tend to feel ashamed, such events (whether actual or inferred) do not cause your feelings of shame. I will explain exactly what I mean by this statement in the next chapter.

3

Irrational Beliefs: the core of shame

I mentioned at the end of the previous chapter that there is a distinction between identifying events about which people feel shame and saying that these events cause shame. In fact, this distinction is crucial and unless you fully understand it, you will be poorly equipped to overcome your shame. Consequently, in this chapter I will discuss the A–B–C model of shame which is the central idea of Rational Emotive Behaviour Therapy (REBT), the approach to counselling I practise and on which the ideas expressed in this book are based.

The A–B–C model of shame

In order to explain the A–B–C model of shame, I will take the example of Marie to whom I first introduced you in Chapter 1. You will recall that Marie felt ashamed of crying in front of her boss when he criticized her unfairly. She felt ashamed about her behaviour because she inferred that it was a weakness. In REBT we often begin by identifying a person's main emotional or behavioural response. This is called a *Consequence* (**C**) for reasons which will become clear later. So, Marie's **C** is shame.

Then we proceed to identify what Marie was mainly ashamed about. This is known as the **A**. In REBT, **A** stands for an *Activating Event*. You will recall from the previous chapter that an Activating Event can be factual or it can constitute an inference – meaning that the event that you think has happened may be factual or may be false; the important point is that you need to check your inference against the available evidence before coming to a conclusion about whether or not it is a fact.

In Marie's case, the relevant **A** can be seen either as her crying in front of her boss or as the inference that she made about this: namely that she revealed a personal weakness by crying. Since it is unlikely that Marie would have felt ashamed if she had inferred that her crying was a strength, we need to incorporate the weakness inference into our account of her Activating Events. Taking this into account, Marie's **A** or Activating Event in this episode is: 'I revealed a weakness to my boss by crying in front of him.'

Now in REBT we urge our clients to assume that their **A** is true, even if it is manifestly false. So, while Marie's friends might try to persuade her that crying in front of one's boss is not a weakness, in REBT we do not at this point do this. This is because we want to identify her beliefs about her **A** which we consider to be at the core of her feelings of shame. The *Beliefs* are known in REBT as **B**.

Why are Beliefs at the core of shame? Let me explain by outlining the possible Beliefs Marie might hold about her **A**, namely: 'I revealed a weakness to my boss by crying in front of him.' There are five possible Beliefs that Marie might hold about this Activating Event. Some of these Beliefs might sound strange, but I need to discuss all of them so that you can understand the Belief that is at the core of Marie's shame. Briefly, the five Beliefs are:

(i)   a met preference;
(ii)   an unmet preference;
(iii) indifference;
(iv) a met demand; and
(v)   an unmet demand.

A met preference

A met preference occurs when you hold a preference about something and you do get what you want. If Marie held a preference that was met by the Activating Event, she would believe: 'I want to show a weakness to my boss by crying in front of him, but I don't have to do so.' If she believes this, Marie will feel pleased because she has succeeded in meeting her preference. As you can see, a met preference is not at the core of shame.

An unmet preference

An unmet preference occurs when you hold a preference about something, but you do not get what you want. If Marie held a preference that was not met by the Activating Event, she would believe: 'I don't want to show a weakness to my boss by crying in front of him, but there is no reason why I must not do so.' If she believes this, Marie will feel disappointed because she has failed to meet her preference, but she is not demanding that she must do so. Again, an unmet preference is not at the core of shame.

Indifference

When you hold an attitude of indifference, you do not care whether or not a particular Activating Event occurs. If Marie was indifferent about the Activating Event, she would believe: 'I do not care whether or not I show a weakness by crying in front of my boss.' If she believes this, Marie will have no feelings about what happened. Thus, it is obvious that an attitude of indifference is not at the core of shame.

A met demand

A met demand occurs when you demand that something must happen and it happens. If Marie held a demand that was met by the Activating Event, she would believe: 'I absolutely must show a weakness to my boss by crying in front of him.' If she believes this, Marie will feel ecstatic because she has succeeded in meeting her demand. As you can clearly see a met demand is not at the core of shame.

An unmet demand

An unmet demand occurs when you hold a demand about something, but you do not get what you believe you must get. If Marie held a demand that was not met by the Activating Event, she would believe that: 'I absolutely must not show a weakness to my boss by crying in front of him.' If she believes this, Marie will feel ashamed because she has done what she believes she must not do. Thus, an unmet demand is the only one of the possible Beliefs that is at the core of shame.

According to the theory of REBT, a demand is irrational because it is rigid, inconsistent with reality, illogical and yields poor emotional and behavioural results. I will discuss this point more fully in Chapter 10. Although it doesn't appear so at first glance, this is true for both met demands and unmet demands. While it is clear that unmet demands lead to emotional problems like shame, you are still vulnerable to emotional problems when you hold a demand that is met because you are not always certain to meet your demands and if you do not then you will experience emotional problems.

To recap, the A–B–C model of shame shows clearly that you do not feel ashamed because of what you do, for example, at **A**, but because of the Beliefs you hold about this **A**. In summary, let me present first in general terms the A–B–C model of shame and then illustrate this model with reference to the case of Marie.

General A–B–C

A = Activating Event, which can be an actual event or an inference (see Chapter 2 for a discussion of the events people feel ashamed about)

B = A demand (which the Activating Event does not meet)

C = Shame

Marie's A–B–C

A = I revealed a weakness to my boss by crying in front of him

B = I absolutely should not have revealed this weakness to my boss

C = Shame

The important role of self-depreciation in shame

So far I have discussed the important role that unmet demands play in shame. In this section I will discuss the role that the irrational Belief known as self-depreciation plays in shame. Some theorists argue that self-depreciation is as important as unmet demands in explaining why you feel ashamed. Others, such as Albert Ellis, the founder of REBT, argue that unmet demands are most important in accounting for shame with self-depreciation coming a close second. Whichever is the case, the important thing for you to remember is that if irrational Beliefs are at the core of shame (as REBT claims) unmet demands and self-depreciation are at the very centre of this core. Let me now consider the attitude of self-depreciation more closely as it relates to shame.

Over the years I have counselled many people with shame problems. From that work and from my review of the psychological literature on shame, it seems to me that when you experience this emotion, you are engaging in one of three types of self-depreciation. The type of self that is portrayed by each I call:

(i)   the diminished self;
(ii)   the defective self; and
(iii) the socially repellent self.

I have already mentioned that shame is a social emotion. What this means when we consider the way that you view your 'self' in shame is that when you feel ashamed you also tend to have a corresponding view of others. Let me deal with each of the selves in turn and as I do so I will discuss how others are viewed.

The diminished self

When you feel shame you may very well say that you feel 'small' or 'insignificant'. Although strictly speaking 'small' or 'insignificant' are not emotions or feelings, as statements they reveal an important point about shame. This point is that in certain situations when you feel ashamed, you experience yourself as diminished. Hence the term 'the diminished self'. As we will see in the following chapter, when you experience shame you 'feel' the judging eyes of your audience upon you and you wish to escape from their gaze. Shrinking the size of your 'self' is one way that you can do this.

If your 'self' is diminished when you feel ashamed then you tend to experience yourself as powerless and you tend to view others as big and powerful. In this type of shame, you may see these big, powerful others as having great control over you which they are likely to exercise. Also, you may experience others as the source of ridicule or scorn or any similar attitude which conveys that they are looking down on you. This sense of being looked down upon is a common feature in people's descriptions when they experience their 'self' as being diminished.

An example of this type of self-depreciation can be found in the case of Rick (see Chapter 1) who felt ashamed and experienced himself as diminished because one of his gang members had let down the reference group with which Rick identified. Correspondingly, Rick experienced others as looking down on him and he said that he felt 'small' while in their presence.

The defective self

Another way in which the self is experienced in shame is as defective. The defective self occurs most frequently when you consider that you have revealed a 'broken' or 'defective' part to a social group that is actually present or psychologically present. If you experience yourself as defective you tend to see relevant others as being flawless. Since they are seen as being without flaws you cannot understand why they would want to associate with a defective person like yourself. You therefore consider that they would want to exclude you from their company. If they have to be present in the same social setting as you (e.g. at a party), you think that they will turn away from you not in disgust (see the next section), but with indifference as if you do not matter to them.

An example of this second type of self-depreciation can be found in the case of Marie who felt ashamed about crying in front of her boss and viewed herself as a weak and defective person for so doing. Correspondingly, she viewed her boss and co-workers (who she feared would discover her defectiveness) as flawless individuals who would seek to exclude her from social interaction.

The socially repellent self

The third way the 'self' is experienced in shame is as socially repellent. If the 'Elephant Man' felt ashamed, this is the way he would have construed himself. If you view yourself as socially repellent when you feel ashamed, you tend to think that others will show disgust towards you in an active way or will turn away from you in disgust. People who are ashamed about bodily blemishes and particularly about bodily deformities tend to view themselves as socially repellent and tend to think that others will be disgusted with them.

An example of this third type of self-depreciation can be found in the case of Bernice (see Chapter 1). Bernice considered that if she showed her body too much then people would discover her shameful secret (that she was sexually abused by her uncle as a child) and would be revolted by her body. Here, it is clear that Bernice considers that she would be socially abhorrent if people were to learn of her secret. If they did discover that she was abused, then Bernice thinks that they would be revolted by her body and turn away from her in disgust.

Bernice also considers herself as defective for not stopping her uncle from abusing her, and correspondingly sees others as flawless beings who would blame her for her failure. The implication is that they would have been able to stop their uncle from abusing them if they were in Bernice's shoes. Bernice's example shows that a person may have more than one type of self-depreciation even in a single episode of shame. These changes of self-depreciation occur as you shift your attention from one aspect of the situation to a different aspect. Thus Bernice considers herself to be defective when she focuses on her past failure to stop the abuse. However, when she focuses on her body as the potential signal of her shame to others she views herself as socially repellent.

Awfulizing and low frustration tolerance

So far I have considered the role of two irrational Beliefs that underpin the emotion of shame: unmet demands and self-depreciation. In REBT theory these irrational Beliefs are considered to be primary determinants of shame. They are thus called primary irrational Beliefs. There are two other irrational Beliefs that have to be considered if you are to achieve a full understanding of the attitudes that underpin shame. Although these two Beliefs need to be considered whenever you feel shame, REBT theory assigns less importance to them when considering the determinants of this emotion. These irrational Beliefs are known as awfulizing and low frustration tolerance and because they are less important than unmet demands and self-depreciation in accounting for shame they are known as secondary irrational Beliefs. Let me consider each in turn.

Awfulizing

Awfulizing has a set of specific meanings in REBT theory which distinguishes it from the loose way it is used in everyday language. When we say it is awful that the weather is bad we do not generally disturb ourselves about the state of the weather. We really mean that the weather is very bad. However, when you feel ashamed and believe, at that time, that it is awful that you have just revealed a weakness you mean the following:

(i)   Revealing the weakness must not be as bad as it is.
(ii) Revealing the weakness is 100 per cent bad.
(iii) Nothing could possibly be worse than revealing the weakness.

However, from my counselling work with those who feel shame, I have discovered that much of the time the reason why they awfulize is because beneath their secondary irrational Belief lie the more primary unmet demands and self-depreciation Beliefs. For example, Marie thought that it was awful that she revealed a weakness to her boss, but when she was asked why it was awful she replied: 'I just believe that I must not show my boss that I have an Achilles heel. If I do that it means that I am a weak, defective person.'

Thus, whenever you feel ashamed and find yourself awfulizing about an Activating Event, it is worth asking yourself whether you are doing so because you hold an unmet demand and/or a self-depreciation Belief. If so, it is likely that these Beliefs are more primary than the awfulizing Belief and better account for the existence of your feelings of shame.

Low frustration tolerance

You can be said to hold low frustration tolerance (LFT) Beliefs about an Activating Event when you believe at that moment that:

(i)   You cannot bear the event.
(ii) You will literally disintegrate if the 'unbearable' event continues to exist; or
(iii) You will forfeit all possibilities of future happiness if the 'unbearable' event continues to exist.

Again, it is my view based on the many clients I have counselled over the years who suffer from shame-related problems that LFT Beliefs in shame are secondary to unmet demands and self-depreciation Beliefs. Thus, if Bernice believes that it would be intolerable to show her body in public, the question is 'Why?' The answer in Bernice's case was that people must not learn that she was sexually abused and that if they found out they would turn away from her because she is so disgusting.

So again, whenever you feel ashamed and find yourself holding an LFT belief about the relevant Activating Event, it is worth asking yourself whether or not this Belief is underpinned by an unmet demand and/or a self-depreciation Belief which according to REBT theory are more primary than the LFT Belief. If so, these Beliefs probably better account for your feelings of shame than your LFT Belief.

Summary

To recap, the REBT viewpoint on shame is based on the A–B–C model of human emotion which states that you feel ashamed (at **C**) when you hold a set of irrational Beliefs (at **B**) about certain Activating Events (at **A**). In the previous chapter, I discussed the type of events about which we tend to feel ashamed. In this chapter, I emphasized the crucial role played by irrational Beliefs (unmet demands, self-depreciation, awfulizing and low frustration tolerance). I stressed that of the four Beliefs, unmet demands and self-depreciation are the most important and can be regarded as the primary irrational Beliefs. However, I also pointed out that while awfulizing and LFT are secondary irrational Beliefs, they still need

23

to be taken into account if a full understanding of the irrational Beliefs which lie at the core of shame is to be achieved.

In the next chapter, I will discuss the relationship between shame and behaviour.

4

Shame and the way you act

In the previous two chapters, I discussed the factors which lead you to feel ashamed. In this chapter, I will consider the relationship between shame and the way you act. In fact, this relationship is quite complex. In my attempt to simplify it, I will distinguish between (i) behaviour that is designed to prevent you from feeling ashamed; (ii) behaviour that you engage in once you have begun to feel ashamed; and (iii) behaviour which is designed to compensate for your feelings of shame.

Acting to avoid feeling ashamed

As humans we have a very strong tendency to avoid physical and mental pain if we can possibly do so. Thus, if we can avoid feeling ashamed we will do so (unless we have a good reason for not doing so). Actually, the fact that we generally act to avoid feeling ashamed means that we hold a set of shame-creating, irrational Beliefs. If we did not hold such beliefs, we would have nothing to avoid. For example, in Chapter 1, I discussed the case of Tom who left his home town after he was badly beaten in a fight. You will recall that he left because he felt deeply ashamed of his beating. One day, several years after the incident, Tom took a long coach journey during which he felt quite content. Owing to a bad accident on the motorway, however, the coach had to make a detour through Tom's old home town. When this was announced over the tannoy system, Tom immediately began to feel anxious and asked the coach driver to set him down before he reached the town, saying that he would make his own travel arrangements.

How can we explain Tom's behaviour? His actions were motivated by the avoidance of shame. Tom's underlying, shame-creating Beliefs remained intact since his beating, but lay dormant as long as Tom kept away from his home town. When the route detour was announced, Tom faced a situation (seeing his home town) which would trigger these dormant Beliefs. In order to prevent these Beliefs from being triggered and to forestall being ashamed, Tom left the coach before it arrived in his old home town. He acted to avoid feeling ashamed.

When we consider the strategies that we tend to use to prevent ourselves from experiencing shame, avoiding others in whose presence we will feel ashamed is perhaps the most frequently used. The reason for this is easily apparent. If you recall, shame is a social emotion. It is experienced when other people are physically present or psychologically present in your mind. We can, with some effort, distract ourselves from thinking of others when we are on our own. This type of distraction is much harder to achieve when we are in the physical presence of others. Given this, we are strongly motivated to avoid being with other people if we think that we will experience shame in such a social context.

Having said this, avoidance as a behavioural strategy to prevent the experience of shame is much broader than social avoidance. We may avoid places, photographs, songs or poems, for example, because they remind us of an experience about which we felt ashamed in the past and about which we may feel ashamed in the present should we be reminded of it. Since virtually anything can remind us of a time when we felt ashamed, it is important that you identify your own triggers for shame-avoidance behaviour. If you succeed in identifying these triggers, you can then identify, challenge and change the irrational beliefs that underpin your dormant shame and which are the reason why you strive to avoid these situations in the first place.

Let me now discuss a number of shame-avoidance behaviours which concern how you relate to others. The first is conformity. Since you tend to experience shame when you reveal something about yourself which is at variance with social mores, one way to avoid experiencing shame is to conform with social customs and the consensus of views that are expressed in your social circle. This means that you will take few risks in expressing your real views or in your behaviour when doing so would put you out on a limb with others. The result is that you tend to be inauthentic when you are with others. They may think that they know you, but they only know your conforming social persona. Your relationships with others, therefore, tend to be fraudulent.

Two other related shame-avoidance behaviours are submissiveness and non-assertiveness. You tend to submit to others and act non-assertively towards them because you predict that if you do not they will criticize you, ridicule you or point out your flaws in public, Activating Events to which you are sure you will react with shame. Rather than take a risk, you submit to other people and keep your true feelings about them to yourself.

A final shame-avoidance strategy that I will discuss here is sycophancy. You may act sycophantly towards someone when you consider that he (in this case) may draw attention to one of your perceived defects, and that if he did you would experience shame. By flattering the person, 'buttering him up' or praising him, you hope to disarm him so that he does not draw attention to your flaw. While you may be successful in stopping him from 'shaming' you (as it appears to you) you hardly feel good about your disingenuousness and you may even feel ashamed about your sycophantic behaviour, particularly if others witness it.

In the next section I will discuss how you tend to act when you have begun to experience shame. Before doing so I wish to stress that behaviour designed to prevent you from feeling ashamed and what you tend to do when you actually feel ashamed are sometimes indistinguishable. The reason for this is quite simple. In both situations, shame-creating irrational Beliefs are involved. When you act to avoid feeling ashamed these Beliefs are dormant, but still have an influence over the way you act. As I said above they must have an influence over your behaviour; otherwise, why would you avoid these situations? However, when you are feeling ashamed, your shame-creating irrational Beliefs are fully triggered and will have a definite influence over your behaviour. Dormant and fully triggered irrational Beliefs are likely to prompt similar behaviour; hence the frequent overlap between shame-avoidant behaviour and shame-activated behaviour. Consequently, when I discuss behaviour such as concealment, denying responsibility, substance abuse and saving one's face by criticizing others – behaviour which is activated by shame – these categories could easily have been included in the present section as behaviour which is designed to prevent the experience of shame. I will remind you of this point as appropriate below.

How you tend to act when you feel ashamed

In psychology it is important to distinguish between an action and an action tendency. An action is a specific piece of behaviour while an action tendency is how you 'feel' like acting without this necessarily turning into an action. You will fully appreciate the importance of this difference when I discuss how to overcome your feelings of shame in Chapters 10 and 11. In this section, I will discuss shame-related action tendencies, i.e. how you tend to behave once you have begun to feel ashamed. Remember, this does not mean that you will definitely act in one or more of these ways; just that you will experience the tendency to do so.

As you read the following action tendencies, why not refer back to the case studies that I introduced in Chapter 1 and see if you can identify which person experienced which action tendency.

Physically withdrawing from others

When you have done something, for example, of which you feel ashamed, and you think that other people have witnessed your behaviour, you will experience a very strong tendency to withdraw physically from the presence of others. This is perhaps the most common action tendency related to shame. The main purpose of physically withdrawing from others when you feel ashamed is to escape their criticism, for example, whether or not they are actually critical of you. As I discussed in Chapter 2, the important thing is that you think (i.e. infer) that they are critical of you.

Averting your eyes from the gaze of others

One of the next most frequently employed forms of shame-activated behaviour is gaze avoidance. If, as the old mystics used to say, the eyes are the gateway to the soul, when you feel ashamed you do not wish others to see into your soul and see what a 'shameful' person you are. If you cannot withdraw from a situation as previously discussed, you can at least partially withdraw from others when they are present. Averting your eyes from their gaze achieves this purpose.

In general, when you avert your eyes from the gaze of others, you have a choice concerning the direction in which you can look. When you feel ashamed, you will most frequently look down. This tendency to look down is in keeping with and deepens the experience of 'feeling small' that people report when they feel shame (see Chapter 3).

In addition to looking downwards, there are other forms of gaze avoidance. These include shielding your eyes from others with your hands and holding your head in your hands. Even here you will still tend to look downwards. This general preoccupation with looking downwards helps to explain why people say things like: 'I hoped that the ground would open up and swallow me.' If you are looking down then you are looking at the ground. People rarely say, 'I hope that the heavens will open up and swallow me' when they feel ashamed.

Isolating yourself from others

When you already feel ashamed, you have a strong tendency to isolate yourself from others rather than to seek out their company or support. There are two major reasons for this. First, when you feel ashamed, you generally hold a self-depreciation Belief. As discussed in Chapter 3, this means that you think that your 'self' is in some way diminished, defective or socially repellent. Under these circumstances you are hardly likely to be in the frame of mind to seek out the support or company of others. Second, as I shall show you in the next chapter, when you feel ashamed you tend to see others as holding a negative attitude towards you. Why would you seek out others if you thought that they would ridicule you, be critical of you or turn their back on you? The answer obviously is: you wouldn't.

Saving face by attacking the other(s) who have 'shamed' you

When you feel ashamed about the way others have treated you, you generally hold what we call in REBT an **A➤C** model of shame. Let's suppose that someone has criticized you in front of a group of

29

your friends and you feel ashamed about his criticism. If you hold an **A➤C** model of shame you think wrongly that the person who criticized you has caused you to feel ashamed. In reality, according to the A–B–C model of REBT your shame is brought about by your irrational Beliefs about his criticism and not by the criticism itself.

However, the **A➤C** model of shame allows you to protect yourself by blaming the other person. If it is the other person's criticism that made you feel ashamed then it is his fault. He is to blame for your shame and not you. This viewpoint enables you to criticize the other person and in doing so you are able to relieve yourself of your feelings of shame. Since blame often involves anger and you tend to feel 'big and powerful' when you are angry, this 'bigness' tends to cover up the feelings of 'smallness' that you experience when you feel shame. In this way you manage to save your own face, albeit temporarily, which you think you have lost when you feel shame.

Attacking the other person allows you to bypass your feelings of shame that have just been activated and thereby you will not experience these feelings to their full extent. However, since bypassing your shame does not allow you to identify, challenge and change the irrational Beliefs that underpin your shame, this action tendency serves to maintain your shame in the long term.

Acting in self-defeating ways

Shame is a painful emotion. Given this fact and your human tendency to escape from painful feelings, we can expect you to attempt to defend yourself from the experience of shame in various ways.

One common way of defending yourself against shame is by imbibing mood-altering substances. This may help to explain the frequency with which the concept of shame is found in the literature on alcoholism and drug dependency. Substance abuse is a good example of self-defeating behaviour that you tend to initiate when you feel ashamed in order to eradicate this emotion. You may, of course, also do so to avoid feeling ashamed in the first place.

Denying responsibility for your actions

Another way in which you attempt to deal with your shame is by denying that you are responsible for your 'shameful' behaviour and by voicing this denial to others. When you tell others that you are not responsible for your actions you think that you cannot be held to account for your actions. Thus, you think that others are not justified in holding a negative opinion of you. The purpose of this type of shame-influenced behaviour is twofold: (i) to stop you from experiencing shame; and (ii) to ward off negative reactions from others.

However, even if you do not consciously experience shame because you have successfully defended yourself in this way, your shame is still in operation. Why would you need to deny responsibility if you did not feel ashamed at some level? The existence of shame that is not consciously experienced is called bypassed shame.

Denying responsibility and communicating this to others is another example of a strategy which can either be employed to prevent you from feeling ashamed in the first place or to quickly eliminate shame once it has been activated.

Concealing verbally and physically

The tendency to hide is very strong once you have begun to feel ashamed. Concealment is a behavioural strategy that people use to avoid the experience of shame in the first place. However, in the same way that bypassed shame motivates denial of responsibility, it also motivates concealment. Why conceal if you are underlyingly not ashamed?

Such concealment can occur verbally or physically. When concealment is verbal you say very little about yourself to others. Thus, you may engage in very little self-disclosure and what you do say about yourself is at a superficial level. Consequently, other people come to see you as bland and superficial and may say that you 'play your cards very close to your chest'.

When concealment is physical you hide aspects of your body from the gaze of others. You do this, of course, because you feel ashamed of yourself for having such aspects. Thus, you may

31

conceal your whole body in very loose-fitting clothes or you may hide specific parts of your body by covering them up or by camouflaging them. A pervasive example of this type of conceal-ment is found, as I have already mentioned, in body dysmorphic disorder (BDD) where a person believes that she is hideously ugly when objectively it is clear that she is not. If you think you may suffer from BDD you will need and can benefit from specialized help, so please consult your GP.

Acting in a way that is consistent with shame

So far I have discussed behaviour that is motivated by shame which seeks to minimize or eradicate this emotion. However, when you feel ashamed, you may also act in a way that is consistent with this emotion. To a very great extent, these behaviours will be self-defeating for you. In effect here you act in ways that are consistent with your self-depreciating attitude. For example, if you feel ashamed about bingeing on unhealthy food you are quite likely to continue bingeing. Since you believe (in this case) that you are a pathetic, weak-willed person, how can you expect yourself to stop bingeing?

The possible number of self-defeating actions that you may enact when you feel ashamed is very great and I will not enumerate them here. If you suspect that you may be acting in a self-defeating manner when you feel ashamed, keep a record of such behaviour and look for the feelings of shame that motivate it. This will help you when I discuss ways of overcoming shame in Chapters 10 and 11. The point to keep in mind is that you are acting in a way that is consistent with your self-depreciating attitude.

Ignoring attempts by others to restore the social equilibrium

When you act in a 'shameful' manner in a social setting, for example, you tend to disrupt the social equilibrium. In response to this, some people present may try to help you to restore this equilibrium. When you feel ashamed you tend to ignore or not respond positively to such attempts. Shame, you will recall, is based to a large extent on a self-depreciating attitude. Because you consider yourself to be insignificant, defective or repellent, this

32

attitude leads you to conclude that you are not worthy of being helped by others and therefore you ignore their restorative attempts. In addition, when you feel ashamed you tend to think that others are critical, rather than supportive of you. Thus, you will tend not to see others' attempts to help you to restore the social equilibrium as helpful. You may well misconstrue them as patronizing sympathy, for example, and ignore them for this and other reasons as a result.

Failing to learn from what 'led' you to act shamefully in the first place

When you feel ashamed for acting in a certain manner, you are not likely to learn any lessons from this episode. The reason for this is simple. Learning from experience requires you to stand back and look at your behaviour in context with as much objectivity as you can muster. When you are ashamed, you are putting yourself down (e.g. viewing yourself as weak) and when you are in this frame of mind you are preoccupied with your intrinsic weakness as a person. Being in this frame of mind, you are hardly able to stand back and objectively ask yourself why you acted in that manner in the first place. Were you to answer this question when you feel ashamed you would tend to reply: 'Because I am such a weak person.' Being in a self-depreciating frame of mind that frequently goes hand in hand with your feelings of shame tends to lead you to take a very blinkered view of the reasons for your behaviour. As we have seen from the above examples, these reasons are very much in line with your attitude towards yourself.

This blinkered view of your behaviour means that you fail to identify the real reasons why you acted in the way that you did. Failing to identify these reasons means that you fail to learn from your experience. And failing to learn from experience means that you will tend to repeat your original behaviour if the circumstances are right. If this happens you will once again feel ashamed and a vicious cycle begins.

As I mentioned at the beginning of this section, there is a difference between action tendencies and actual behaviours. The former do not have to be transformed into the latter. However, when actual tendencies become actions and you practise these actions so that they become habitual, the result is that you entrench your feelings of shame and make it very difficult for yourself to overcome your shame. This is why acting against shame-related action tendencies is such an important part of overcoming your feelings of shame, as I will discuss in Chapters 10 and 11.

What you do to compensate for feeling ashamed

When your behaviour is designed to compensate for your feelings of shame, you tend to act in a way that is a direct opposite to what you really feel about yourself. To illustrate this, let's take the case of Tom who I introduced in Chapter 1. If you remember, Tom was a very short man who privately thought of himself as a wimp. To compensate for this view of himself and for the feelings of shame that stemmed from it, Tom acted in a variety of macho ways. He pumped iron, learned martial arts with the intention of picking fights with and beating up men taller than himself. He also revelled in picking up and seducing women taller than himself. His goal was to prove to others and to himself that he was a real man despite his lack of stature.

Unfortunately, such attempts to compensate for one's shame are rarely a long-term solution to experiencing shame. One day you will not be able to compensate for your feelings of shame and you will not have the skills to overcome these feelings. As a result, your self-constructed charade will collapse and you will be flooded with shame. This is exactly what happened to Tom. If you recall, one day he picked on the wrong man and got badly beaten up. No longer able to compensate for his shame, Tom left his home town for good so that he wouldn't have to face people after his beating, so badly flooded with shame was he after this event.

In the next chapter, I will turn my attention to the relationship between shame and the way you think.

5

Shame and the way you think

In this chapter I will discuss the relationship between shame and the way you think. First I will outline how you tend to think once you are experiencing shame. In particular, I will contrast this type of thinking with that which leads to shame in the first place. Then, I will discuss thinking which is designed to prevent you from feeling ashamed even though you have underlying shame-creating irrational Beliefs.

How you tend to think when you feel ashamed

In this section, I will consider how you tend to think once you have begun to feel ashamed. As I will show you, this type of thinking is somewhat different from the thinking that leads you to feel ashamed in the first place. I discussed this latter type of thinking in Chapters 2 and 3. I showed you in those chapters that shame is the result of you making one or more of a set of inferences at **A** (in the A–B–C framework) and holding a set of irrational Beliefs at **B** about these inferences at **A**.

Shame-related inferences include: (i) thinking that you have fallen short (and most frequently very short) of your ideal; (ii) thinking that you have let down your reference group; (iii) thinking that you have been let down by a member of your reference group; and (iv) thinking that others are judging you negatively whether or not you think you merit such judgement. On their own, these inferences are not sufficient for you to feel shame. In order for you to feel ashamed, you bring a set of irrational Beliefs to these inferences. These beliefs are unmet demands, some form of self-depreciation, awfulizing and low frustration tolerance (see Chapter 3 for a full discussion of these irrational Beliefs).

When you experience shame you then tend to think in a number of distorted ways. Your feelings of shame and the irrational Beliefs that underpin them literally influence your subsequent thinking. In this section I will draw upon the case of Marie discussed in Chapter 1 to illustrate most of my points. The following are typical examples of shame-influenced thinking.

(1) Overestimating the 'shamefulness' of your behaviour

Because Marie was ashamed of crying in front of her boss after he criticized her, she subsequently overestimated the 'shamefulness' of her behaviour and saw her crying as a great weakness.

(2) Overestimating the extent to which others will notice your 'shameful' behaviour

When your 'shameful' behaviour is not readily noticeable, but you feel ashamed about it, you subsequently think that others will notice your behaviour more than you would if you were not ashamed of how you acted.

(3) Overestimating the likelihood that others will regard your behaviour as 'shameful'

Because Marie was ashamed of crying in front of her boss, she subsequently overestimated the likelihood that her boss (and others that he might tell of the incident) considered her behaviour to be 'shameful'.

(4) Overestimating the extent to which others will regard your behaviour as 'shameful'

Because Marie was ashamed of bursting into tears in front of her boss, she subsequently overestimated the extent to which her boss and others who might have learned of the incident regarded her behaviour as 'shameful'. As a result Marie thought that others viewed her behaviour as a great weakness.

(5) Overestimating the length of time that others will remember your 'shameful' behaviour

Because Marie was ashamed of crying in front of her boss, she subsequently overestimated the length of time that others would remember her behaviour. In her case, she thought that they would remember it forever.

(6) Overestimating the likelihood that others will regard you as 'shameful'

Because Marie was ashamed of shedding tears in front of her boss, she subsequently overestimated the likelihood that her boss and others who learned of the incident would regard her as a weak, shameful person.

(7) Overestimating the extent to which others will regard you as 'shameful'

Because Marie was ashamed of crying in front of her boss, she subsequently overestimated the extent to which her boss and others who found out about the incident would regard her as a weak, shameful person. Consequently, she inferred that they would regard her as a thoroughly weak, pathetic person.

(8) Overestimating the length of time others will regard you as 'shameful'

Because Marie felt ashamed about losing control in front of her boss, she subsequently overestimated the length of time that her boss and others who learned about the incident would regard her as a weak, shameful person. Thus, Marie thought that they would think this way of her forever.

(9) Overestimating the likelihood that those observing will tell others about you

Because Marie felt ashamed about shedding tears in front of her boss, she overestimated the likelihood that her boss would tell others of the incident. Thus, she thought that her boss would definitely tell others that she burst into tears after he criticized her.

(10) Exaggerating what those observing will tell others about you

Because Marie felt ashamed about crying in front of her boss, she subsequently exaggerated what she thought her boss would tell others about the incident. Thus, she thought her boss would tell others that she completely fell apart during their interview.

37

(11) Exaggerating the extent to which others will ridicule you

Because Marie felt ashamed about bursting into tears in front of her boss, she subsequently exaggerated the extent to which others would ridicule her for crying before her boss. Thus, when she thought of the scene where her boss told others about what had happened, she imagined in her mind's eye that they would all have a really good laugh at her expense. Also, when she next went into work she thought that her co-workers were sniggering behind her back about the incident.

(12) Exaggerating the extent to which others will exclude you

Because Marie felt ashamed about shedding tears in front of her boss, she exaggerated the extent to which others would exclude her. Thus, she thought that they would not ask her to social occasions like having a drink in the pub after work and that she would not be welcome at the firm's Christmas party.

(13) Exaggerating the extent to which others will feel sorry for you

When you feel ashamed about your behaviour and you don't think that others will ridicule you, you may well subsequently think that they will feel sorry for you. Rather than thinking that they will feel sorry for the situation that you find yourself in, you tend to think that they will pity you as a person.

(14) Overestimating the likelihood that you will behave 'shamefully' in the future

Because Marie felt ashamed of crying in front of her boss, she subsequently overestimated the likelihood that she would behave 'shamefully' in the future. Thus, Marie thought that every time her boss wanted to see her, she would burst into tears.

(15) Exaggerating the 'shamefulness' of your future 'shameful' behaviour

As I discussed earlier, when you feel ashamed about your behaviour, you tend subsequently to overestimate the likelihood that you will act 'shamefully' in the future. You will also tend to exaggerate the 'shamefulness' of this behaviour. Thus, you will rarely think that you might act in a mildly (or even moderately) 'shameful' manner. Rather, you will tend to think that your future behaviour will be very shameful.

(16) Overestimating the likelihood that you will act on your 'shameful' thoughts

I mentioned in Chapter 2 that one of the things that you may feel ashamed about is your thoughts. If this happens then you subsequently think that you are much more likely to act on these thoughts than if you do not feel ashamed of thinking them. For example, people who are ashamed of having aggressive thoughts think they are more likely to act on these aggressive thoughts than those who are disappointed, but not ashamed of such thoughts.

If you feel ashamed of your thoughts, you tend to demand that you must not have such thoughts. Your attempt to banish once and for all such thoughts from your mind only serves to keep these thoughts, and this anxiety combines with your original shame and leads you to conclude that if you can't stop your 'shameful' thoughts you will act on them.

A small minority of people who are ashamed of their aggressive thoughts do, in fact, act on them. If you think that this applies to you, you may need professional help. Contact your doctor and discuss your concerns with him or her.

In this section I have shown you that once you start to feel ashamed, this emotion and the irrational Beliefs which underpin it lead you subsequently to develop a range of inferences which significantly distort reality. Shame, then, encourages you subsequently to think in a variety of exaggerated ways where you overestimate the likelihood of negative events occurring and you exaggerate the seriousness of these events. Then these shame-influenced inferences become your new A's in the A–B–C framework and these A's tend to trigger new shame-related irrational Beliefs with the result that your feelings of shame become intensified. Such deepened feelings of shame then lead to the production of more grossly distorted inferences at **A** which then trigger more shame-related irrational beliefs.

When you feel ashamed, then, you are in danger of setting up a vicious cycle of distorted inferences, irrational Beliefs and increasingly intensified feelings of shame. This is why it is important to work on overcoming your feelings of shame as soon as you begin to experience them. If you do so successfully, then you will undercut this vicious circle before it begins to take hold. I will show you how to overcome your feelings of shame in Chapters 10 and 11.

Thinking designed to prevent or get rid of shame

In this section, I will discuss modes of thinking which are designed either to prevent you from experiencing shame or to get rid of shame once you have started to experience it. As I discussed in the previous chapter, in both situations you hold shame-creating, irrational Beliefs. Since the types of thinking are very similar in both situations, I will discuss them in one section. Before I do so, however, I wish to stress that I am not advocating that you use these modes of thinking as long-term solutions to your shame. Far from it. As I will discuss in Chapters 10 and 11, the best long-term way of overcoming shame is to identify, challenge and change the irrational Beliefs that underpin your feelings of shame.

However, you do need to understand that you may well use ways of thinking which are designed to help prevent or rid yourself of your feeling of shame and which may give you short-term relief even if they do not constitute a longer-term solution to the problem of shame. In the spirit of furthering such understanding, I will discuss four such types of thinking.

Denying responsibility for your actions

Shame is based on the idea that you accept responsibility for your actions. Thus, one way of preventing or getting rid of shame is to deny that you have such responsibility. If we take the example of Marie first introduced in Chapter 1, Marie can prevent or get rid of her shame about crying in front of her boss by thinking: 'The reason why I cried in front of my boss was because I wasn't myself.' If

Marie 'wasn't herself' how can she be expected to take responsibility for her actions? And if she cannot be expected to accept responsibility for her actions, she will not depreciate herself and therefore she will not experience shame. As I discussed in the previous chapter, you may also deny responsibility in public statements to others.

Blaming others in your mind

When you feel ashamed (or are likely to feel ashamed) about what another person may have said to you, about you or about how that person may have treated you, you can prevent or get rid of your shame by blaming the other person in your mind. If you blame the other person in your mind you will shift your attention away from yourself and on to that other person. Remember that shame is based on self-depreciation. Thus, if you can get away from depreciating yourself by depreciating the other person in your mind, you will prevent or get rid of shame. You will, of course, feel angry instead, but for many people (but by no means all) anger is a more acceptable and less painful emotion than shame. Thus, if Marie thinks that her boss is to blame for her tears (e.g. 'My boss is a rotten person for making me cry') she will feel anger rather than shame. As I will discuss in Chapter 6, you may act on such over-blaming by criticizing the other person directly or indirectly to others.

Compensatory thinking

Another way of preventing or getting rid of shame is by thinking things that serve to compensate for your shame. Since shame is based on self-depreciation, a common form of compensatory thinking involves you viewing yourself as a great or noble person. Thinking that you are much better than another person who would otherwise in some way trigger the Beliefs underpinning your feelings of shame is also a common form of compensatory thinking.

It is important to note that frequently you do not really believe such compensatory thoughts. Indeed, deep down you really believe the opposite – that you are a shameful person. But such compensatory thoughts do serve a purpose – to prevent or get rid of shame in the short term.

An example of compensatory thinking would be if Marie thought that she was a great person for crying in front of her boss because her tears show how wonderfully sensitive she is. This thought is compensatory because she really believes that she is a weak, 'shameful' person for breaking down in response to his criticism. I discussed behaviour which compensates for feelings of shame in the previous chapter.

Avoidant thinking

A very common form of preventing yourself from experiencing shame in the first place and getting rid of shame in the second place is to avoid thinking about whatever you feel (or are likely to feel) ashamed of. This frequently involves you thinking about something other than what you feel ashamed about. Distracting yourself from your shame by attending to other features of your environment is a related form of avoidant thinking. This form of thinking is rarely successful in anything other than the very short term and is not a good long-term way to overcome feelings of shame.

In this chapter I have discussed shame and the way you think. In the next chapter, I will review some of the material that I have presented so far in this book as I show you why, by and large, shame is an unhealthy emotion.

6

Why shame is unhealthy

So far in this book I have discussed what we tend to feel ashamed about, the irrational Beliefs that are at the core of shame and the relationship between shame and the way we act and think. I hope you have seen why shame is an unhealthy negative emotion. If not, in this chapter I will spell out the reasons why I believe that shame is, on the whole, unhealthy. While shame is a painful emotion, this pain, on its own, is not an indication of an unhealthy emotion. In Rational Emotive Behaviour Therapy (REBT), we distinguish between healthy and unhealthy negative emotions, but both are experienced as painful. So pain on its own is not a good indicator of whether an emotion is healthy or not. Rather better indicators are the Beliefs which underpin emotions. In REBT, healthy negative emotions stem from rational Beliefs while unhealthy negative emotions stem from irrational Beliefs. As such, shame is seen in REBT as an unhealthy negative emotion since it is based on irrational Beliefs. However, the unhealthy aspects of shame can be seen more clearly when we look at its effects.

When you feel shame you tend to act in self-defeating ways

As I discussed in Chapter 4, when you feel ashamed you tend to act in self-defeating ways. Thus, when you feel ashamed you tend to do the following:

(i)   You tend to avoid social contact with people and isolate yourself from them.

(ii)   You tend to attack others in order to save face.

(iii) You may abuse mood-altering substances in order to rid yourself of the pain of shame.

(iv)   You tend to let others know that you are not responsible for your 'shameful' behaviour.

(v)   You tend to conceal important aspects of yourself from others with the result that you develop only superficial relationships with them.

(vi)   You tend to increase the chances that you will act 'shamefully' in the future because your feelings of shame interfere with you learning from experience.

(vii)   You tend to ignore attempts by others to restore the social equilibrium.

(viii) You tend to act in a variety of ways that are designed to compensate for your shame but which are ultimately self-defeating.

You tend to act in self-defeating ways to prevent yourself from feeling ashamed

In Chapter 4, I discussed the fact that as humans we are strongly motivated to avoid emotional pain. Thus, in order to prevent yourself from experiencing shame, you tend to act in ways that are self-defeating. Although these behaviours may be successful in this respect, at least in the short term, they are not helpful to you in the long term. Also, you act in such ways because you are still underlyingly ashamed. It is just that your shame-creating, irrational Beliefs have not been fully triggered. In order to prevent yourself from feeling shame:

(i)   You tend to avoid situations which remind you of your shame.

(ii)   You tend to conform to the wishes of your social group even though you may not agree with the group.

(iii)   You tend to act submissively and non-assertively with others whom you think have the power to 'shame' you.

(iv)   You tend to act in a sycophantic manner to people who you
        again think have the power to 'shame' you.

(v)   You may also use most of the behavioural strategies discussed
        in the previous section in order to prevent yourself from
        feeling ashamed.

Your shame leads to unproductive results for others

Your feelings of shame do not have unhealthy results only for you.
They may have unproductive results for those with whom you come
into contact through the way you treat them. There are two major
ways that others suffer from behavioural manifestations of your
shame.

(i)   When you feel ashamed you may attack those people who, in
        your eyes, are responsible for your feelings of shame. The
        result is that they may well attack you back and your
        relationship with them will ultimately deteriorate which will be
        bad news for you and for them. These others may experience
        both unhealthy anger and shame when you attack them and
        become disconnected from you as a result of the ensuing and
        escalating conflict.

(ii)   Your shame means that you will develop superficial relation-
        ships with others. This will have unproductive results for those
        who like you and wish to get to know you better, but whose
        efforts you rebuff.

When you feel shame you distort things in negative ways

As I discussed in Chapter 5, when you feel ashamed, this feeling and
the irrational Beliefs that underpin it lead you to make overly
negative distortions of reality. Thus, when you feel ashamed you
tend to overestimate the frequency, intensity and duration of others'
negative reactions towards you. Believing these inferences to be
true, you then act on them (as described above) and tend to behave

towards others in a variety of dysfunctional ways (e.g. you may avoid them, submit to them or attack them).

You tend to think in dysfunctional ways to prevent yourself from feeling ashamed

I also described in Chapter 5 various ways of thinking that are designed to help prevent yourself from feeling ashamed. It is important to realize that you employ the following modes of thinking only because you hold a set of shame-creating ideas which would otherwise be activated with the result that you would fully experience feelings of shame.

(i)   Denying to yourself that you are responsible for your actions.

(ii) Blaming others in your mind.

(iii) Thinking that you are a great person. This is an example of compensatory thinking designed to keep shame at bay.

(iv) Avoiding thinking about an event of which you would otherwise feel ashamed.

The irrational Beliefs that underpin your shame will lead you to be vulnerable to other unhealthy negative emotions

Shame does not exist in an emotional vacuum. The irrational Beliefs that are at the core of your feelings of shame render you vulnerable to other unhealthy negative emotions such as anxiety, depression, guilt and unhealthy anger. When you feel ashamed about your behaviour, for example, you may also feel anxious about others learning about the way you have acted. Your anxiety is underpinned by similar irrational Beliefs that underpin shame such as: 'Other people absolutely must not find out about my behaviour. If they do they will despise me and this will prove that I am a despicable person.'

In Chapter 3, I explained that self-depreciation is a primary irrational Belief that underpins shame. If you depreciate yourself, for example, when you fall very short of your ideal, then you may very well depreciate yourself when you fail at a very important task and when you break your moral code. In the former case you will feel depressed and in the latter case you will experience guilt. It is not inevitable that you will hold depression- and guilt-creating self-depreciating Beliefs if you hold shame-creating self-depreciating Beliefs, but you will certainly increase the chances of doing so if you feel ashamed of yourself.

Finally, there is an increasing psychological literature linking shame with unhealthy anger. This is especially the case in marital arguments. In a typical argument, the husband (in this case) criticizes his wife who feels ashamed about his criticism. To cover up her shame so that she does not feel its full impact she makes herself angry about what he has just said and criticizes her husband back. He feels ashamed about her attack on him and to cover up his shame he redoubles his attack on her and makes an even more angry criticism of her. His wife then responds by a further angry criticism of him.

In this way, shame and unhealthy anger interact to produce a potentially destructive argument which may in certain cases lead to physical violence. Here unhealthy anger is an attempt to protect you from your shame. It may be successful in this respect in the short term but, in doing so, unhealthy anger often causes more problems than it solves. For a fuller discussion of unhealthy anger see my book *Overcoming Anger* (Sheldon Press, 1994).

Why shame is unhealthy: another look at the case histories

So far I have discussed why shame is unhealthy in fairly general terms. Since we can only clearly see that shame is unhealthy by examining its effects on real people, let us now return to the case examples that I first introduced in Chapter 1 to see the effect that shame had on the people described in those cases.

Marie

Marie's shame about crying in front of her boss was unhealthy because it led her to make a number of negatively distorted inferences which in turn led her to act self-defeatingly. This is what I said about the effect of Marie's shame on her subsequent thinking and behaviour in Chapter 1:

> In her state of shame, Marie began to think that her boss would look down on her for crying, that he would tell everyone in the office who would then either look down on her or pity her. She thought that everyone would hear about this incident and would remember it forever. She resolved there and then to avoid her boss as much as possible and especially when she was upset, and decided from that moment to keep to herself when it came to dealing with her work colleagues.

This is a very clear statement of the unhealthy consequences stemming from Marie's feelings of shame.

Elise

Elise felt ashamed about having erotic dreams about another woman which she inferred meant that she was a lesbian. Elise's feelings of shame again led her to distort reality and act self-defeatingly. Thus, she tried to avoid being in the presence of women and when she had to be with them she avoided looking at them. These attempts at avoidance only increased the frequency and 'shamefulness' of her forbidden thoughts which in turn encouraged Elise to believe that she would become an outcast from her religious community if anyone even suspected her shameful secret. As you can see, Elise's shame hardly led to healthy consequences for her.

Rick

Rick felt ashamed about one of the members of his gang 'grassing' on another member to the police. Because Rick felt ashamed he kept a very low profile in his local community.

Consequently, he led a very restricted life and felt bored and listless as a result.

Tom

Tom felt ashamed about being beaten up in a fight. So strong were his feelings of shame that he decided to leave his home town and could not even return years later when a coach on which he was travelling had to be rerouted through the town. He disembarked from the coach as soon as he learned the nature of the detour.

Bernice

Bernice felt ashamed about letting her uncle sexually abuse her as a child. She also thought that her body would reveal her shame. Because she felt shame, she developed sexual problems which led to the breakdown of her marriage. She would not reveal any part of her body in case others would discover her 'shameful' secret and be revolted by her.

Mohammed

Mohammed felt ashamed about bringing his local Muslim community into disrepute by forging signatures on other people's credit cards which he had stolen to fund his impulsive spending habits. As a result of his feelings of shame, Mohammed refused to see people who wanted to visit him in prison and seriously considered giving up his Muslim faith which had been so important to him. He also thought that he would be treated like a pariah on his release from prison.

Sarah

In Sarah's case, first discussed in Chapter 1, her shame problem was not centred on any specific event. Rather, her feelings of shame related to many different events. Consequently, she avoided many situations that could have given her pleasure. Because she had a strong tendency to avoid social situations dating back to early childhood, Sarah did not acquire basic social skills – something which reinforced her tendency to avoid other people. Sarah's case shows that people who are particularly prone to shame and avoid social situations as a result often get into the following typical vicious cycle.

Feeling ashamed, they are prone to avoid other people, which deprives them from learning appropriate social skills. Lacking these social skills, they are reluctant to approach other people. If they do so, they tend to have less satisfactory contact with others than they would if they had good social skills. From their distant vantage point, such people observe others as having good social contact with one another which reinforces the shame-based idea that they are defective. This then promotes more avoidance of others, etc., etc.

Situational shame and shame-proneness

People tend to experience shame in specific situations. These may be actual situations as when, for example, Marie felt ashamed about revealing a weakness by crying in front of her boss. However, such situations may be held in one's mind's eye. They may reflect actual situations – as when, for example, Marie feels ashamed when she thinks back and recalls crying in front of her boss – or they may reflect situations that have not occurred. For example, Marie may feel ashamed about thinking about crying in front of her boss, even though this event has not yet occurred.

What these examples have in common is that they all refer to specific situations rooted in time and space. As such I call the shame that is experienced in such situations: situational shame. Most of the case studies that I introduced in Chapter 1 and briefly reviewed earlier in this chapter (with the exception of Sarah) are examples of situational shame. Now it may be the case that Marie, Elise, Rick and the others experienced shame across a broad range of situations. However, we do not know this. All we know is that they experienced shame in given situations and can therefore be said to have experienced situational shame.

As I have shown earlier in this chapter when I considered the effects of situational shame, it is clear that such shame is unhealthy. However, since it is linked to specific situations, situational shame is less destructive than what has been called trait shame, but which I call high shame-proneness (HSP). If you have high shame-proneness, it is likely that you will experience shame in many different situations. HSP will also lead you to avoid many situations in which you would otherwise experience shame. Thus, even if you do not actually experience shame, your life will be significantly affected for the worse if you have HSP. The case of Sarah, first introduced in Chapter 1 and discussed again earlier in this chapter, is a good example of someone who is highly prone to shame.

In conclusion, while situational shame will have a deleterious effect on specific areas of your life, if you are highly prone to shame then your life will be marked either by the pain of shame or by the restrictive effects of an avoidant lifestyle.

Some objections to the idea that shame is unhealthy

So far in this chapter I have argued that shame is an unhealthy negative emotion and have carefully detailed some of its major unhealthy consequences. However, not everybody considers shame to be an unhealthy negative emotion. Some people think that shame helps us to regulate our social behaviour and that without the controlling effects of shame we would run riot and act in socially inappropriate ways. These critics argue that without shame we would be shameless and it is this state of shamelessness that is unhealthy. For such people, shame protects us from the ravaging effects of shamelessness.

These critics may have a point if the only alternative to shame is shamelessness. However, as I will argue in the following chapter, there is a healthy alternative to shame. Briefly, I call this alternative to shame 'disappointment' and it is healthy because (i) it is based on a set of rational Beliefs (you will recall from Chapter 3 that shame is based on a set of irrational Beliefs); and (ii) it encourages healthy behaviour and functional modes of thought (you will recall from

Chapters 4 and 5 as well as from the early sections of this chapter that shame leads to self-defeating behaviour and unproductive modes of thought). Since I will discuss this issue fully in the next chapter I will not elaborate on these points here.

Another argument that people use in favour of the idea that shame is healthy is based on the notion that shame comes in two forms: healthy shame and unhealthy shame. Such an argument is usually circular in that it is healthy when it has healthy effects and it is regarded as unhealthy when it has unhealthy effects. The problem with this argument is that you are usually given no way of distinguishing between healthy and unhealthy shame other than its effects. It is possible that the shame you feel on one occasion may be psychologically identical to the shame you might experience in another situation, but its effects may be different and these effects may be due to factors out of your control.

For example, imagine that you feel ashamed about shouting at your young son in front of a friend and you indicate your shame by holding your head in your hands. If your friend puts her arms around you, you may well get over your shame because she has shown compassion for your situation. The above critics may regard your shame here as healthy because it has yielded a productive response. But they may well regard the same experience of shame as unhealthy if your friend had scolded you – a response which would have resulted in you feeling even more ashamed.

The problem with this position is twofold. First, it relies on factors outside of your control to determine the health (or otherwise) of your feelings of shame. Your shame is healthy if other people, for example, respond favourably towards you; and, conversely, your shame is unhealthy when it elicits a negative response from others. Second, this response again does not consider the idea which is at the heart of this book, namely that shame is based on a set of irrational Beliefs and leads to predominantly negative consequences for the individual that is within that person's control (i.e. the way she tends to act and think once she feels shame) and that its healthy alternative (i.e. disappointment) is based on a set of rational Beliefs and leads to more constructive ways of thinking and behaving.

The final objection to the idea that shame is unhealthy is contained in the argument that shame is productive because it tells you that there is something wrong that requires attention. While it is true that shame does function as a signal in this respect, it is, in fact, a very poor signal. Thus, when Marie feels ashamed about crying in front of her boss in response to his criticism of her, her shame does signal to her that there is something that requires attention (that she has displayed a weakness in public), but it does not help her to address this issue. In fact her feelings of shame will discourage her from thinking how to better handle criticism from her boss in future because her mind will be focused on what a weak, defective person she is for crying in the first place. In contrast, as I will discuss in the next chapter, disappointment also serves as a signal that something is wrong, but it encourages the person to pinpoint the problem to be addressed in Marie's case (i.e. how to better handle her boss's criticism) without the interfering effects of self-depreciation.

So far in this book, I have discussed the nature of shame and its effects. We are now ready to consider more fully the healthy alternative to shame. This will be the focus of the next chapter.

7

Disappointment: the healthy alternative to shame

The first step to overcoming shame is to understand what is the healthy alternative to this emotion. Towards the end of the previous chapter, I argued that the absence of shame or shamelessness is not a good alternative to shame. In this chapter, I will argue that disappointment is the healthy alternative to shame (I will explain why this is the case more fully in Chapter 9). Since disappointment is a direct alternative to shame, we tend to feel disappointed about the very things that we feel ashamed of. In later chapters, I will point out what differentiates shame from disappointment.

Disappointment and the language of emotions

In my book on anger entitled *Overcoming Anger* (Sheldon Press, 1994), I pointed out that we do not have good words in the English language to differentiate between anger that is basically unhealthy and anger that is basically healthy. Some people have called the former 'anger' and the latter 'annoyance', but this is unsatisfactory because most people consider annoyance to be milder than anger and to be about less negative, aversive Activating Events. For a healthy negative emotion to be a good alternative to an unhealthy emotion, it has to be of equal intensity and about the same Activating Event. To ensure that these two criteria were met, in *Overcoming Anger* I used the terms 'unhealthy anger' and 'healthy anger' to refer to the two different types of anger.

We are faced with exactly the same problems with shame. We just do not have in the English language a suitable word to denote the healthy alternative to shame. To try and help me find such a word, I asked a number of the country's leading experts in the psychology of emotion and in the fields of counselling and psychotherapy for their views on this matter. Several practitioners remarked that they would be happy to use whatever terms their clients considered to be healthy alternatives to shame. While I have a certain sympathy with this view and would be happy to apply it in the consulting room, clearly it is unacceptable in a book such as this. For we could find thirty different terms, say, used by every hundred readers. In this book, therefore, I do have to settle on one term that can be used consistently as a healthy alternative to shame.

Three possible terms were mentioned by my group of experts. Some proposed the term 'healthy shame' which could then be contrasted with 'unhealthy shame'. The problem for me in using the terms 'healthy shame' and 'unhealthy shame' centres on the central role that self-depreciation plays in shame. Since self-depreciation almost always occurs in shame, there is a danger that in striving to achieve 'healthy shame' you may not work to minimize your attitude of self-depreciation. Consequently, you would still be vulnerable to 'unhealthy shame'. To me, then, shame without self-depreciation is a contradiction in terms.

A second term that was suggested by another group of experts was 'regret'. The problem with the term 'regret' as the healthy alternative to shame is that it is also used as the healthy alternative to guilt. Since it is important to differentiate between shame and guilt, we need a term which suggests a healthy alternative to shame but which does not also suggest a healthy alternative to guilt. For this reason, I decided not to use 'regret' as the healthy alternative to shame in this book.

This left the third term which was suggested by another group of experts: 'disappointment'. I have decided to use this term as the healthy alternative to shame in this book although it is not without its problems. The main difficulty with this term is that it is used where shame is not an issue. Thus, you can apply for a job and feel disappointed that you were not successful. If you experienced an unhealthy negative emotion about this failure it would not necessarily be shame unless you thought you were revealing a weakness to others and you consequently engaged in self-depreciation.

However, the term 'disappointment' does share the difficulties that regret and healthy shame have as the healthy alternative to shame. First, it tends not to be used as a healthy alternative to guilt (as regret is). Second, when you feel disappointment you tend not to engage in self-depreciation (if you recall, this was the problem with healthy shame).

Let me stress one final important point with respect to the use of disappointment as the healthy alternative to shame. Although disappointment sounds like a mild emotion, it can vary in intensity from mild to severe. Thus, if you feel very ashamed of your behaviour, the healthy alternative is to feel very disappointed about it. Healthy negative emotions tend to match their unhealthy counterparts in intensity and it is important that you remember this in subsequent chapters. Thus, if your shame is strong (moderate or mild), strong (moderate or mild) disappointment is the healthy alternative to strive for.

What do we feel disappointed about?

As I will discuss in the following chapters, what distinguishes disappointment from shame (at **C** in the A–B–C framework) is the Beliefs that you hold at **B** about the relevant Activating Event at **A** and how you tend to think and act when you experience these different emotions. What is common to both shame and disappointment is what you feel ashamed and disappointed about at **A**. Thus, you feel disappointed about the very same things you feel ashamed about. The difference between shame and disappointment, let me reiterate, lies primarily at **B**, not at **A**. We tend to think and act in different ways when we feel these different emotions.

When we feel disappointment, it is usually because we make a number of inferences at **A** which may or may not be correct (reread Chapter 2 for a full discussion of inferences). These inferences are what you feel disappointed about. Let's go back to the people first presented in Chapter 1, but this time let's assume that they all felt disappointed, but not ashamed. Note that they felt disappointed about the very things they felt ashamed about.

(1) Marie felt disappointed about crying in front of her boss because she considered that she had publicly revealed a weakness.

(2) Elise felt disappointed about her sexual feelings because she inferred that she was a lesbian.

(3) Rick felt disappointed when Geoff 'grassed' to the police because he considered that Geoff (i) broke the gang's code of honour; and (ii) showed his gang in a bad light in the local community. Remember that Rick closely identified with his gang.

(4) Tom felt disappointed when he inferred that being beaten up revealed him as a wimp in the eyes of those who witnessed the beating and of those who might learn about it in the future.

(5) Bernice felt disappointment about her body because she inferred that it revealed that she had been sexually abused and as a result others would conclude that she was a shameful person and treat her accordingly.

These examples illustrate common issues about which you feel disappointment. Remember that when you feel the emotion of disappointment you do not tend to distinguish between actual events and inferences. To you, your inferences are actual events, full stop. Thus, in the fourth example above, Tom does not consider his inference that he will be viewed by others as a wimp as anything other than a fact.

What are the common issues that you feel disappointed about? Let me now outline them in general terms. They are, of course, the same issues about which you feel ashamed.

Falling short (and often very short) of your ideal

You tend to feel disappointed when you fall short of your ideal particularly when this occurs in a social context or is related to some kind of social code. The word 'social' is important here in that disappointment, when it is an alternative to shame, is very much a 'social' emotion. As I will discuss presently, disappointment occurs either when others are present or when the presence of others is in the forefront of your mind when you are alone reflecting on something you have done, for example.

As I discussed in Chapter 2, shame occurs most often when you think you have fallen *very* short of your ideal. When you think rationally about such a 'fall from grace' you will feel disappointment rather than shame. Here is a list of events (actual or inferred) about which you tend to feel disappointed.

(1) Behaviour

First, under this heading, you can feel disappointed about what you do. Examples are:

(i) You infer that you have revealed a weakness (e.g. Marie could healthily feel disappointed when she cried in front of her boss).

(ii) You infer that you have acted in a way that breaks an important social code (e.g. you remain seated when the national anthem is played at a public gathering).

Second, under this heading you can feel disappointed about what you failed to do. Examples are:

(i) You have failed to act honourably (e.g. you infer that you have failed to go to the aid of someone who needs help).

(ii) You infer that you have failed to act in a way that observes an important social convention (e.g. you inadvertently do not wear appropriate attire at a formal event).

(2) Thoughts and images

Under this heading, you feel disappointed about finding yourself thinking thoughts or having images which you deem to be forbidden, but which do not necessarily violate your moral code (e.g. Elise could healthily feel disappointed about having thoughts which she infers means that she is a lesbian).

(3) Emotions

Here you feel disappointed about experiencing emotions which you consider to be anti-ideal. Thus, you may have as your ideal feeling loving kindness for your enemies, whereas in reality you feel murderous towards them. Your murderous rage constitutes your anti-ideal about which you feel disappointed.

(4) Bodily blemishes and deformities

Here you consider that part of your body is blemished or deformed in some way and this blemish or deformity (e.g. a visible scar, a very long nose or a small penis) is something which constitutes an anti-ideal. In helping a person with body dysmorphic disorder (BDD), she (in this case) is encouraged to feel disappointed, but not ashamed of an aspect of her body which she regards as a defect, but which others in reality consider within normal limits. The person is not initially helped to think that her defect is not a defect when she is ashamed of it. Once she feels a healthy negative emotion about this 'defect', she is in a better frame of mind to re-evaluate this inference.

Letting down your reference group

The second category of events about which you tend to feel disappointment as a healthy alternative to shame concerns your inferences that you have let down your reference group and shown that group in a bad light. In modern parlance, you have brought that group 'into disrepute'. A reference group is, if you recall, any grouping of people with whom you closely identify. An example of this category is provided by the case example of Mohammed discussed in Chapter 1. Mohammed could be helped to feel disappointed, but not ashamed about letting down his family, local community and religious reference groups by his criminal actions.

Being let down by a member of your reference group

The third category of events that you may feel disappointed about (as opposed to ashamed of) concerns not your own behaviour, but the behaviour of a member (or members) of your reference group. An example of this category is represented by the case of Rick (see Chapter 1). Rick could be helped to feel disappointed, rather than ashamed about Geoff (i) breaking the gang's code of honour; and (ii) showing his gang in a bad light in the local community.

Being a reflection of how others treat you and/or think about you when you haven't done anything to merit such behaviour and/or attitude

In this category you can feel disappointed rather than ashamed about the way others treat you and/or think about you when you haven't done anything to merit their behaviour and/or attitude. An example of this is found in the case of Bernice who was helped to feel disappointment rather than ashamed about being sexually abused by her uncle. In doing so, she stopped viewing this act as a stimulus to self-evaluation.

Being exposed to the judgement of others

I mentioned earlier that disappointment (when it is a healthy alternative to shame) is a social emotion. This means that you tend to feel disappointed (and ashamed) when you are in the actual presence of other people or when you think of the responses of others when you are alone.

While you mostly feel ashamed and disappointed when other people are present to witness your 'shameful' behaviour, for example, the actual presence of others is not a necessary condition for the experience of these emotions. You can and do feel ashamed and disappointed when you are on your own, thinking about the way you acted. When you do this, however, you do have other people in mind. Thus, others do need to be present psychologically rather than physically for you to experience disappointment and shame when you have acted 'shamefully'.

When you feel disappointed (or ashamed), you infer that others who may be actually or psychologically present are judging you in some negative way. More specifically, you infer that they either look down on you or will shun you in some way.

Summary

In this chapter, I have discussed what people tend to feel disappointed about. I made the point that we tend to feel disappointment and shame about the same things. Thus, you feel disappointed and ashamed when you fall short, and most often very short of your ideal; when you let down your reference group; when you are let down by a member of a reference group; when others treat you or think of you as meriting shame when in fact you do not; and when others look down on you or shun you either in your mind or in reality. I also stressed that you feel disappointed about such matters whether they are actual or inferred events. The important point is that you consider them to be actual events.

However, while these constitute events about which you tend to feel disappointed, such events (whether actual or inferred) do not cause your feelings of disappointment. As with shame, the core of disappointment lies in the Beliefs you hold about these events. I will discuss this fully in the next chapter.

8

Rational Beliefs: the core of disappointment

I mentioned in the previous chapter that there is a distinction between identifying events about which people feel disappointed and saying that these events cause disappointment. In Chapter 3, I applied the A–B–C model to shame. I will apply the same A–B–C model to explain what really determines your feelings of disappointment. In doing so, you will begin to see what you will need to change if you are to overcome your feelings of shame.

The A–B–C model of disappointment

In order to explain the A–B–C model of disappointment, I will take the example of Marie to whom I first introduced you in Chapter 1. You will recall that Marie felt ashamed of crying in front of her boss when he criticized her unfairly. She felt ashamed about her behaviour which she saw as a weakness. However, in this chapter, I will assume that Marie felt disappointed about crying in front of her boss even though she saw it as revealing a weakness.

You will recall from Chapter 3 that in REBT we often begin by identifying a person's main emotional or behavioural response. This is called a Consequence (**C**). So, Marie's **C** is disappointment.

Then we proceed to identify what Marie was mainly disappointed about which you will remember is known as the Activating Event (**A**). In Chapter 2, I pointed out that an **A** can be factual or it can constitute an inference, meaning that the event that you think has happened may be factual or it may be false; the important point is that you need to check your inference against the available evidence before coming to a conclusion about its truthfulness.

In Marie's case, the relevant **A** can be seen either as her crying in front of her boss or as the inference that she made about this: namely that she revealed a personal weakness by crying. In this case, Marie's **A** or Activating Event in this episode is: 'I revealed a weakness to my boss by crying in front of him.'

I stressed in Chapter 3 that in REBT we urge our clients to assume temporarily that their **A** is true, even if it is manifestly false. So, while you might try to persuade Marie that crying in front of one's boss is not a weakness, in REBT we do not at this point do this. This is because we want to identify her Beliefs about her **A** which we consider to be at the core of her feelings of disappointment. You will recall that these Beliefs are known in REBT as **B**.

Why are Beliefs at the core of disappointment? Let me explain by repeating three of the five possible Beliefs Marie might hold about her **A**. Remember that Marie's **A** is: 'I revealed a weakness to my boss by crying in front of him.' The five possible Beliefs are:

(i)   a met preference;
(ii)   an unmet preference;
(iii)   indifference;
(iv)   a met demand; and
(v)   an unmet demand.

Here, I will discuss the three Beliefs that are relevant to us at this stage. These are: (i) indifference; (ii) an unmet demand; and (iii) an unmet preference. For a discussion of the remaining two, see Chapter 3.

Indifference

When you hold an attitude of indifference, you do not care whether or not a particular Activating Event occurs. If Marie was indifferent about the Activating Event, she would believe: 'I do not care whether or not I showed a weakness by crying in front of my boss.' If she believes this, Marie will have no feelings about what happened. Thus, it is obvious that an attitude of indifference is not at the core of disappointment.

An unmet demand

An unmet demand occurs when you hold a demand about something, but you do not get what you believe you must have. If Marie holds a demand that was not met by the Activating Event, she would believe: 'I absolutely must not show a weakness to my boss by crying in front of him.' If she believes this, Marie will feel ashamed because she has done what she believes she must not do. As I stressed in Chapter 3, an unmet demand is at the core of shame. It cannot, therefore, be at the core of disappointment.

An unmet preference

An unmet preference occurs when you hold a preference about something, but you do not get what you want. If Marie holds a preference that was not met by the Activating Event, she would believe: 'I don't want to show a weakness to my boss by crying in front of him, but there is no reason why I must not do so.' If she believes this, Marie will feel disappointed because she has failed to meet her preference, but she is not demanding that she do so. Thus, an unmet preference is at the core of disappointment.

To recap, the A–B–C model of disappointment shows clearly that you do not feel disappointment because of what you do, for example at **A**, but because of the Beliefs you hold about this **A**. In summary, let me present in general terms the A–B–C model of disappointment and illustrate this model with reference to the case of Marie.

General A–B–C

A = Activating Event, which can be an actual event or an inference (see Chapter 7 for a discussion of events people feel disappointed about)
B = A preference (which the activating event does not meet)
C = Disappointment

Marie's A–B–C

A = I revealed a weakness to my boss by crying in front of him
B = I don't want to show a weakness to my boss by crying in front of him, but there is no reason why I must not do so
C = Disappointment

The important role of self-acceptance in disappointment

So far I have discussed the important role that unmet preferences play in disappointment. In this section I will discuss the role that the rational Belief known as self-acceptance plays in disappointment. Some theorists argue that self-acceptance is as important as unmet preferences in explaining why you feel disappointment. Others, such as Albert Ellis, the founder of REBT, argue that unmet preferences are most important in accounting for disappointment with self-acceptance coming a close second. Whatever the case, the important thing for you to remember is that if rational Beliefs are at the core of disappointment (as REBT claims) unmet preferences and self-acceptance are at the very centre of this core. These Beliefs are rational because they are (i) flexible; (ii) consistent with reality; (iii) sensible; and (iv) conducive to you experiencing healthy emotions and acting in your own and others' best interests (see Chapter 10 for a fuller discussion of this point). Let me now consider the attitude of self-acceptance more closely as it relates to disappointment as a healthy alternative to shame.

The first point that we need to address concerns the definition of the 'self'. Paul Hauck in his book, *Hold Your Head Up High* (Sheldon Press, 1991) has provided a very simple but profound definition of the self. He says that the self is 'every conceivable thing about you that can be rated'.

Human beings cannot legitimately be given a single global rating

Hauck's definition of the 'self' is one that I agree with and one that I will use in this book. According to this definition, all your thoughts, images, behaviours and bodily parts are part of your 'self'. Furthermore, we do not only have to include all these aspects from the day you were born to the present day, but also all those aspects that will exist from the present to the moment you die. This means that your 'self' is incredibly complex and defies being assigned a legitimate single rating.

Note that you do rate your 'self' when you feel ashamed. Thus, when Marie feels ashamed about crying in front of her boss, she believes that she is a weak, defective person for doing so. Here she is not only rating her behaviour as weak; she is also assigning a single negative global rating to her 'self' or personhood (i.e. she rates herself as a weak, defective person).

If Marie were to feel disappointed but not ashamed about crying in front of her boss, she might still consider her behaviour to be weak, but she would not rate her 'self'. Rather she would accept herself as an unrateable person who has acted weakly.

Note that in REBT we are not necessarily against you rating aspects of yourself. Indeed, such ratings can be productive. Thus, if Marie rates crying in front of her boss negatively, she will be motivated to overcome this perceived problem. In fact, her disappointment-related self-acceptance will also aid her in over-coming this problem since it will help her to concentrate her energies on the problem at hand. However, if she rates her crying *and* her 'self' negatively, as is the case if she were to feel ashamed about her behaviour, then her shame-based, negative self-rating will interfere with her attempts to overcome her crying problem. When Marie feels ashamed about her behaviour, she will be preoccupied with her global defectiveness and therefore not be able to concentrate on overcoming the problem at hand.

If you put into practice the idea that you cannot legitimately assign yourself a single rating, you will not experience shame, for shame is based on the notion that your 'self' is rateable. Thus, in Chapter 3, I pointed out that when you feel ashamed you view your 'self' as diminished, defective or socially repellent. However, when you feel disappointed but not ashamed you do not rate yourself. Rather, you accept yourself as an unrateable person who may have fallen short of your ideal, revealed a weakness or displayed an unsightly deformity to others.

Let's see how this principle works in practice by applying it to the cases of Rick, Marie and Bernice. If you recall, in Chapter 1 Rick felt ashamed because he viewed himself as diminished because one of his fellow gang members had let down this reference group with which Rick identified. In order to feel disappointed instead, Rick needs to resolve not to rate himself on the basis of how his fellow gang member acted, although it is healthy for him to dislike this person's behaviour.

Second, let's take the case of Marie who felt ashamed about crying in front of her boss because she viewed herself as a weak and defective person for so doing. In order to feel disappointed instead, Marie needs to consider herself as a complex individual who defies a single rating, but she should dislike revealing a weakness to her boss if that's how she views crying in front of him.

Third, let's consider Bernice who felt ashamed about anyone learning that she was sexually abused in childhood by an uncle because she viewed herself as socially abhorrent. However, if Bernice were to accept herself as an unrateable person who cannot be defined either by her uncle's abuse of her or by the adverse reaction of anyone who discovered her secret, she would feel very disappointed but not ashamed about these events.

Human beings are essentially fallible

If you have an essence as a human being surely it is that you are fallible. The rational psychiatrist, Maxie C. Maultsby, Jr, has vividly encapsulated this essential nature of human beings by saying that all human beings have an incurable, error-making tendency. We are programmed, if you will, to make mistakes and even when we learn from our errors we are still able and often do make the same errors all over again. The best you can hope for, therefore, is to minimize your errors, for you certainly cannot eradicate them. This means that at times you may well fall short (and, yes, often very short) of your ideal. If you accept yourself as a fallible human being when this happens, even though others may look down on you, then you will feel disappointed but not ashamed.

All humans are equal in humanity, but unequal in their different aspects

The noted British clinical psychologist, Professor Paul Gilbert, has said that the concept of ranking is important to our understanding of shame. This means that when we feel ashamed we tend to rank ourselves below others in terms of worth. Thus, as I argued in

Chapter 3, if you consider your 'self' to be diminished, you tend to see relevant others as big and powerful. Ranking also plays an important if different role in our understanding of disappointment as a healthy alternative to shame. When you feel ashamed about revealing a weakness in public, you rank your 'self' below the 'selves' of others in terms of worth. However, when you feel disappointed, but not ashamed about revealing this weakness, you rank yourself below others on this point alone. You do not see your 'self' as less than the 'selves' of others. Rather, you see that you are equal to them in humanity though unequal on the point of revealing that weakness at that time under those conditions. The concept of self-acceptance, therefore, permits ranking of aspects of ourselves in relation to the same aspects of others, but it actively discourages the ranking of people in terms of differing worth.

If you apply this principle in practice, you do not see people as more powerful than you, nor do you see them as perfect. Rather, you see them as fallible human beings like yourself who can also act in ways that fall very short of their ideals, who can also reveal weaknesses and act in ways in public to which others may respond with disgust. In essence, you consider that you and they are united in your humanity. This is in stark contrast to the alienation you experience when you feel ashamed; for when you experience shame, you feel alienated from others rather than united with them.

Unconditional self-acceptance avoids errors of overgeneralization

When you accept yourself unconditionally as a person, you avoid errors of overgeneralization. Consider Marie who, if you recall, felt ashamed of crying because she believed that she was a weak, defective person for doing so. If we accept, for the moment, that Marie's tears are a weakness and a defect, for her to conclude that her whole 'self' is weak and defective on the basis of that particular weakness and defect is an example of overgeneralization or what philosophers call 'the part-whole error'. This means that a person, in this case, Marie, judges the whole of her 'self' on the basis of a part of herself. When you accept yourself, you avoid committing this illogical error. Thus, if Marie accepted herself she would conclude that even if crying in front of her boss constituted a weakness and a defect, she would still be a fallible human being whose 'self' defied a single rating. This conclusion is logical and does not constitute the part-whole error. Marie would still be disappointed if she reached this latter conclusion because of her related unmet preference: 'I would prefer not to have cried in front of my boss, but there is no reason why I absolutely should not have done so.'

Unconditional self-acceptance is based on a preferential philosophy

If you recall, in Chapter 3, I showed you that when you feel ashamed you are depreciating your 'self' in some way. I also showed you that this self-depreciating belief stems from a demanding philosophy. This is illustrated in Marie's case: 'I must not display a weakness by crying in front of my boss and because I have done what I absolutely should not have done, I am a weak, defective person.' This belief led Marie to experience shame.

As the last statement in the previous section shows, unconditional self-acceptance is related to disappointment because it stems from a preferential philosophy; in Marie's case: 'I would prefer not to display weakness by crying in front of my boss, but there is no reason why I must not do so. If I do it is undesirable, but it only proves that I am an unrateable, complex, fallible human being who has acted undesirably.' This belief would lead Marie to experience disappointment, but not shame.

Anti-awfulizing and high frustration tolerance

So far I have considered the role of two rational Beliefs that underpin the emotion of disappointment as a healthy alternative to shame: unmet preferences and self-acceptance. In REBT theory, these rational Beliefs are considered to be the primary determinants of disappointment. They are thus called primary rational Beliefs. There are two other rational Beliefs to consider if you are to achieve a full understanding of the attitudes that underpin disappointment as a healthy alternative to shame. Although these two Beliefs do need to be considered whenever you feel disappointment, REBT theory assigns less importance to them as determinants of this emotion. These rational Beliefs are known as anti-awfulizing and high frustration tolerance and because they are less important than unmet preferences and self-acceptance in accounting for disappointment they are known as secondary rational Beliefs. Let me consider each in turn.

Anti-awfulizing

Anti-awfulizing in REBT means that you rate something as 0 per cent to 99.99 per cent bad on a scale of badness and you recognize that nothing can be worse than 99.99 per cent bad. Anti-awfulizing is best expressed by something that Smokey Robinson's mother used to say to her son: 'From the day you are born till you ride in the hearse, there's nothing so bad that it couldn't be worse.'

When you feel disappointed but not ashamed about revealing a weakness, for example, you believe that it is bad that you have done so, but it is not terrible. However, you are able to hold this rational Belief because you have not demanded that you absolutely should not have revealed the weakness and you have accepted yourself as a complex, unrateable fallible human being for so doing. Thus, your anti-awfulizing Belief tends to stem from your unmet preference and your self-acceptance Belief.

High frustration tolerance

You can be said to hold high frustration tolerance (HFT) Beliefs about revealing a weakness, for example, when you believe at that moment that:

(i)   You can bear revealing the weakness;
(ii) You will not disintegrate if you continue to reveal this weakness and/or if people continue to remember this event; and
(iii) You will still experience future happiness even though you may continue to reveal the weakness or if people continue to remember it.

70

As with anti-awfulizing Beliefs, you tend to hold these high frustration tolerance Beliefs because you hold an unmet preference about revealing the weakness and you accept yourself for doing so.

To recap, the REBT viewpoint on disappointment as a healthy alternative to shame is based on the A–B–C model of human emotions which states that you feel disappointed (at **C**) when you hold a set of rational Beliefs (at **B**) about certain Activating Events (at **A**). In the previous chapter, I discussed the type of events about which you tend to feel disappointed. In this chapter, I emphasized the crucial role played by rational Beliefs in disappointment. Specifically, I discussed four rational Beliefs (unmet preferences, self-acceptance, anti-awfulizing and high frustration tolerance). I stressed that of the four Beliefs unmet preferences and self-acceptance are the most important and can be regarded as primary rational beliefs. However, I also pointed out that while anti-awfulizing and HFT are secondary rational Beliefs they still need to be taken into account, if a full understanding of the rational Beliefs which lie at the core of disappointment as a healthy alternative to shame is to be achieved.

In the next chapter, I will discuss why disappointment is a healthy alternative to shame and show how disappointment influences the way you act and subsequently think once you have begun to experience this emotion.

9

Why disappointment is the healthy alternative to shame

In Chapter 7, I argued that disappointment is the healthy alternative to shame, but I did not fully explain why this is the case. In this chapter, I will devote myself to this issue.

You do not need to defend yourself against or compensate for disappointment

In Chapters 4 to 6, I discussed how a propensity to feel shame may lead you to adopt many defensive manoeuvres against experiencing the full force of this unhealthy negative emotion. I also showed how this same propensity may lead you to adopt a number of strategies designed to help you to compensate for this emotion. The main reason why you attempt to defend yourself against or compensate for feeling ashamed is that you hold a set of irrational Beliefs that underpin this emotion. In particular, you hold one or more unmet demands and one or more self-depreciating Beliefs about a certain class of events (see Chapter 2 for a review of what events we tend to feel ashamed about).

However, when you feel disappointed but not ashamed about these same events, you do not hold these unmet demands or self-depreciating beliefs. Rather, as I discussed in Chapter 8, you hold one or more unmet preferences and one or more self-accepting Beliefs. Holding these rational Beliefs means that there is no reason to defend yourself or to compensate for feeling disappointment. Let me provide a personal example to illustrate what I mean.

This is the second time that I have written this book. The first time, I had almost finished it when I failed to observe a basic rule of computing (save and back-up everything that you write) and promptly lost the entire manuscript. I recognized that I had acted very stupidly and had thus fallen very short of my ideal, but I did not demand that I absolutely should not have done what I did, nor did I depreciate my 'self'. Consequently, I did not feel ashamed. If I had the Beliefs that I just outlined and experienced shame as a result, I would have sought to defend my 'self' by blaming the machine, for example, or by telling people that I lost the manuscript in a way for which I could not be held accountable. Also, if I felt ashamed, I would not be telling you about it now!

The reason why I did not feel the urge to defend myself and why I can tell you about my stupid behaviour is that I felt disappointed, but not ashamed about what I did. I felt this way because I believed (and still believe) the following: 'I really wished that I hadn't acted so stupidly, but there is no law forbidding me from so doing. I am a fallible human being who is prone to error and I can accept myself as such.'

I hope you can see, then, that if you hold a set of rational Beliefs (and in particular, one or more unmet preferences and self-acceptance ideas) about falling very short of your ideal, for example, then the disappointment that you will feel will not lead you to make excuses for why you behaved as you did, nor will it lead you to compensate for your behaviour. Rather, as I will show later, your feelings of disappointment and the rational Beliefs that underpin them will encourage you to take responsibility for your actions and to learn from your errors. This is what I did. I now ensure as far as is humanly possible that I save and back-up everything that I write. I say 'as far as is humanly possible' because I recognize that being human I am not immune from making the same mistake again. If I did, I would endeavour to take the same view of it as I did the first time.

How you tend to act when you feel disappointed

In Chapters 4 and 6, I pointed out that when you feel ashamed you then tend to act in a variety of self-defeating ways. This is not the case when you feel disappointed. Rather, when you feel disappointment but not shame you tend to act in a variety of healthy ways. A list of these behaviours will now follow.

Remaining in the presence of others

When you have done something, for example, about which you feel disappointed but not ashamed, and you think that other people have witnessed your behaviour, you will not experience a very strong tendency to withdraw physically from the presence of others. Rather, you will tend to remain in their presence since you do not disturb yourself about any criticisms they may make of you.

Holding the gaze of others

When you feel disappointment but not shame in the presence of others, you will still tend to retain eye contact with these others. Since you do not 'feel small', there is no reason for you to look away from them even if they are critical of you. Nor will you experience the urge to shield your eyes from others with your hands or hold your head in your hands. As noted in the previous chapter, when disappointment is the healthy alternative to shame it is based on the principle of parity where you and others are equal in humanity, but unequal in certain aspects. Since you regard yourself as equal to others present when you feel disappointment, even though you have acted in a way that falls very short of your ideal, there is no reason for you to avert your eyes from their gaze.

Remaining in contact with others

When you feel disappointed rather than ashamed, you tend to seek out the company or support of others rather than isolate yourself from them. There are two major reasons for this. First, when you feel disappointed rather than ashamed, you generally hold a self-acceptance Belief. As discussed in Chapter 8, this means that you think that your 'self' is fallible rather than diminished, defective or socially repellent. Under these circumstances, you are likely to be in the frame of mind to seek out the support or company of others rather than isolate yourself from them. Second, when you feel disappointed rather than ashamed, you tend to see others as holding a sympathetic attitude towards you for your plight unless you have clear evidence to the contrary. As such, you will tend to move towards them rather than away from them.

Disclosing when it is appropriate to do so

When you feel disappointed but not ashamed, you make sensible judgements about what to disclose to others about yourself. This is in direct contrast with shame which leads to wide-ranging concealment. Since disappointment leads to judicious disclosure, others close to you 'feel' that they know you.

When you feel disappointed but not ashamed about some aspect of your body, you are prepared to reveal this aspect of yourself in relevant situations. You do not engage in the wide-ranging concealment or camouflage which stems from shame and which is the breeding ground for the development of body dysmorphic disorder (see Chapter 4).

Responding to attempts by others to restore the social equilibrium

When you act in a 'shameful' manner in a social setting, for example, you tend to disrupt the social equilibrium. In response to this, some people present may well try to help you to restore this equilibrium. When you feel disappointed but not ashamed about your actions, you tend to respond positively to such attempts. Disappointment, you will recall, is based to a large extent on a self-accepting attitude. Because you accept yourself as a fallible human being and thus you do not consider yourself insignificant, defective or repellent, this attitude leads you to conclude that you are worthy of being helped by others and therefore you respond to their restorative attempts. In addition, when you feel disappointment but not shame, you tend to think that others are supportive rather than critical of you. Thus, you will tend to see others' attempts to help you restore the social equilibrium as helpful rather than as patronizing sympathy, for example.

Learning from your actions

When you feel disappointed but not ashamed for acting in a certain manner, this feeling will motivate you to learn any lessons from this episode. The reason for this is simple. Learning from experience allows you to stand back and look at your behaviour in context with as much objectivity as you can muster. When you are disappointed but not ashamed, you are accepting yourself rather than putting yourself down (as you do when you feel ashamed). This attitude frees you to concentrate on what you did and why you did it. In other words, disappointment facilitates objectivity and curiosity about your behaviour in addition to motivating you to act differently in future similar circumstances.

In contrast, shame allows you to become preoccupied with your intrinsic weakness as a person which will interfere with you standing back and objectively asking yourself why you acted in that manner in the first place.

How you tend to think when you feel disappointed

In this section I will discuss how you tend to think once you have already begun to feel disappointed rather than ashamed. This type of thinking should be distinguished from the thinking that leads you to feel disappointment in the first place. I discussed this latter type of thinking in Chapters 7 and 8.

When you feel disappointed you tend to think in a number of realistic ways. I will again draw upon the case of Marie to illustrate these points, but this time I will assume that Marie felt disappointed rather than ashamed of crying in front of her boss. The following are typical examples of disappointment-influenced thinking.

(1) Viewing information revealed in a compassionate self-accepting context

Once you have acted in a way that falls far short of your ideal, for example, and you feel disappointed but not ashamed about this behaviour, you can then stand back and view that behaviour in a compassionate self-accepting context. Thus, if Marie feels disappointed but not ashamed about crying in front of her boss, she is then able to consider that behaviour compassionately and consider it to be an unfortunate response rather than a weakness, for example.

Viewing her behaviour in a compassionate context will also mean that Marie will make realistic judgements about her future behaviour. She will not overestimate the extent to which she will behave 'shamefully' with her boss in the future, nor will she make such judgements about her behaviour in other areas.

(2) Thinking realistically about the likelihood that others will notice or be interested in your behaviour

When you feel ashamed, you tend to think that others will be very interested in what you have done. However, when you feel disappointed but not ashamed about your behaviour, you will acknowledge that others will have a range of reactions to your behaviour. Thus, when Marie feels disappointed but not ashamed about crying in front of her boss, she will think that some people will show a great deal of interest in her behaviour, others will show moderate or mild interest and yet others will be uninterested in what she did.

(3) Thinking realistically about the degree of disapproval you will receive for your behaviour

When you feel disappointed but not ashamed about your behaviour, you will tend to think realistically about the degree of disapproval you will receive for that behaviour. Thus, when Marie feels disappointment but not shame about crying in front of her boss, she will consider that others will display a range of responses towards her behaviour. A minority, she will think, will disapprove greatly of her behaviour, considering it to be great weakness. Others, she will acknowledge, will mildly disapprove of her crying while yet others, she will assert, will consider her behaviour to be a strength rather than a weakness.

In addition, when Marie feels disappointed rather than ashamed about her behaviour, she will also think that others will have a variety of responses towards her as a person.

(4) Thinking realistically about the length of time any disapproval will last

When you feel disappointed but not ashamed about your behaviour, you will tend to think realistically about the length of time that people will disapprove of you for your behaviour. Thus, when Marie feels disappointed but not ashamed about shedding tears in front of her boss, she will appreciate that it is very unlikely that he and others who might learn of the incident will disapprove of her for very long, if she thinks that they will disapprove of her at all. If she does consider that any disapproval she receives will last a long time, she will acknowledge that very few people will hold such a lasting opinion of her.

I hope that I have shown you that disappointment is a healthy alternative to shame, even if this emotion is very strong. I have argued that in contrast to shame, disappointment leads to realistic thinking and functional behaviour which is designed to keep you involved with others (rather than separate from them) and to encourage you to take responsibility for your behaviour and to learn from it.

As I shall discuss in the following two chapters, acknowledging that disappointment is the healthy alternative to shame is an important initial step that you need to take if you are to overcome your shame problem.

10

How to overcome situational shame

In Chapter 6, I made a distinction between situational shame and shame-proneness. By situational shame, I mean the shame you experience in a given situation, while by shame-proneness I mean a more general tendency to experience shame across a fairly large number of situations. In this chapter, I will focus on how you will overcome situational shame, i.e. the shame that you experience in a given situation; while in the following chapter, I will address myself to how you can become less shame-prone. However, it is important that you read and study this chapter carefully if you are shame-prone since you still need to deal with situational shame.

I will now provide a step-by-step guide to overcoming situational shame and in doing so I will use Marie's problem where she felt ashamed about crying in front of her boss for illustrative purposes. While the steps are presented in a logical order, please do not think that this order is inflexible. However, I do suggest in the first instance that you follow the steps as presented before you make any changes to this order.

Step 1: Acknowledge that you felt ashamed in the situation to be analysed and that this emotion is unhealthy

This step may be obvious, but it is worth stating since it is easy to think you have experienced shame when, in fact, you may have experienced guilt or embarrassment. A good way of distinguishing shame from guilt is to realize that guilt occurs when you have broken (or failed to live up to) a moral code and consider yourself to be a bad person, while in shame you have fallen well short of a non-moral standard and consider yourself to be a diminished, defective or socially repellent person for doing so. In shame you are also more preoccupied with how others view you than you are in guilt.

Shame can also be distinguished from embarrassment in that the

79

latter is more short-lived than shame and is usually about momentary lapses in socially appropriate behaviour while shame is about more serious breaches of a social code. When you feel ashamed you usually engage in self-depreciation which lasts longer and is more well-defined than the fleeting self-depreciation that can occur in embarrassment. Indeed, you do not have to depreciate yourself when you feel embarrassed. Thus, you may well feel embarrassed when someone pays you a compliment and not depreciate yourself at all. Finally, you are much more likely to blush when you feel embarrassed than when you feel ashamed.

Once you have identified your feeling as shame rather than guilt or embarrassment, for example, you can check that shame is the correct feeling, by considering how what you felt influenced your subsequent thinking and tendencies to act. You might find it helpful to reread Chapters 4 and 5 for a review of how shame affects your thinking and behaviour. In reviewing this material, it is likely that you will see that shame is unhealthy in that it has self-defeating consequences and affects your relationships with others in negative ways. If you are not convinced that your feelings of shame are unhealthy, then you might like to review Chapter 6 where I discuss this very point.

Marie was fairly certain that she felt ashamed about crying in front of her boss. She knew that her feeling was shame because of the following action tendencies and thoughts that typically stem from shame. First, Marie 'felt' like hiding her face in her hands and hoped that the ground would open up and swallow her. Second, she thought that others would look down on her if they found out about the incident. These reactions persuaded Marie that she felt ashamed and that this feeling was unhealthy and that she needed to overcome it.

Step 2: Choose a specific example of your situational shame and be as concrete as you can

By definition, situational shame is shame that is experienced in a given situation. However, since it is very easy for you to think about this situation in vague terms, it is important that you be as concrete as you can when analysing your chosen example. The more concrete you can be about this specific example, the more accurate you will be in identifying the irrational Beliefs that underpin your feelings of shame. And the more accurate you are in identifying these irrational Beliefs, the more successful you will be in challenging and changing them.

As previously stated, Marie chose the situation where she felt ashamed about crying in front of her boss as the example to be analysed.

Step 3: Acknowledge that disappointment is a healthy alternative to shame

In committing yourself to overcoming your situationally based feelings of shame, it is important that you see clearly what is the healthy alternative to shame. In Chapter 7, I argued that disappointment is the healthy alternative to shame and it is important for you to consult that chapter if you have any doubts that you will be working towards feeling disappointed rather than ashamed about the situation under investigation. Once you have identified disappointment as the healthy alternative to shame and have committed yourself to this emotion as the goal towards which you will be working, you can proceed to the next step.

Marie acknowledged that feeling disappointed about crying in front of her boss was a realistic and healthy alternative to feeling ashamed. She could see that feeling disappointment would have none of the negative consequences of shame, but would help her to understand why she was crying in the first place. Since shame would lead Marie to become preoccupied with matters such as her defectiveness and other people's critical attitude towards her, she concluded it would not help her to stand back and consider objectively the reason for her tears.

Step 4: Accept yourself for feeling ashamed

Before you start to analyse the concrete example that you have selected, it is important that you answer the following question. Do you feel ashamed of or depreciate yourself for feeling ashamed in

81

the first place? If so, it is important that you deal with this matter before proceeding further. This may be a strange concept, but my years of experience as a counsellor have taught me that people frequently depreciate themselves for the way that they feel. If you think that you may have depreciated yourself for feeling ashamed, then unless you deal with this issue, you will be preoccupied with feeling ashamed about feeling ashamed rather than be focused on understanding and overcoming your original shame. However, if putting yourself down for feeling ashamed is not a problem for you, you may proceed to Step 5.

What do you need to do if you are putting yourself down for feeling ashamed? First, it is important that you realize that while shame is an unhealthy negative emotion, it is a very common one and it is experienced to a greater or lesser extent by all humans. This means that you are not an abnormal human being for experiencing shame. Rather, you are very fallible for having this emotional response. Second, even though you may see your experience of shame as a weakness or as a defect, this does not mean that you are weak or defective as a person. Your feelings of shame are only a part of you and cannot define you. Third, when you feel ashamed about feeling ashamed, you are demanding that you must not feel ashamed in the first place. However, the reality was that you did experience this emotion and if there was a law of the universe decreeing that you must not feel shame then you wouldn't have felt it nor could you have. Therefore, there is no such law.

Marie recognized that she felt ashamed for feeling ashamed about crying in front of her boss. She overcame this secondary shame by not demanding that she absolutely shouldn't have felt her original feelings of shame, while retaining her preference not to do so. Furthermore, she accepted herself as a fallible human being, who is not exempt from feeling ashamed.

Accepting yourself for feeling shame in the first place will then help you to address the issues that led you to have this experience so that you can feel disappointment instead.

Step 5: Identify what you felt most ashamed about at **A** and assume temporarily that it is true

You are now ready to identify what you were most ashamed about in the concrete episode that you have selected to analyse. For example, if you were Marie you could ask yourself: 'What was it about crying in front of my boss that I was most ashamed of?' If you are stuck on this point, refer back to Chapter 2 where I listed the inferences that people make when they experience shame. Marie considered the most shameful thing about crying in front of her boss was that she revealed a weakness before him. The aspect of the situation that you are most ashamed of is known as the Critical **A**. So Marie's Critical **A** is: 'I revealed a weakness in front of my boss by crying in front of him when he criticized me.'

After you have identified your Critical **A**, it is very important for you to treat it as though it were true, at least for the time being. The reason that this is important is that it allows you to identify the irrational Beliefs that are at the core of your feelings of shame. If Marie reassesses her feelings of **A** at this point and concludes, for example, that it isn't really a weakness to cry in front of her boss, she will stop feeling ashamed, but she will not have done so by identifying, challenging and changing her shame-creating, irrational Beliefs – which in REBT we argue is the better, longer-term solution to her shame problem. If Marie stops feeling ashamed by reinterpreting a weakness as a strength, for example, she will tend to feel ashamed when she later reverts to thinking of her crying (or any behaviour) as a weakness. So at this point, resist any temptation you may feel to reinterpret your Critical **A**.

Step 6: Understand that your feelings of shame stem largely from irrational Beliefs and are not caused by **A**

It is a basic principle of Rational Emotive Behaviour Therapy that Activating Events or Critical **A**s, to be more precise, contribute to but do not cause your feelings and behaviour at point **C** in the A–B–C framework. Rather, the ways you feel and act depend largely (but not exclusively) on the Beliefs you hold about these As. Thus, it is important that Marie fully embraces the view that her feelings of shame about revealing a weakness in front of her boss (which is, if you recall, an inference) depend on the irrational Beliefs she holds about doing so and not on this inference alone.

If you are not convinced that your feelings of shame are determined largely by irrational Beliefs, please reread Chapter 3.

Step 7: Identify your irrational Beliefs and discriminate them from their rational alternatives

After you have accepted the point that your feelings of shame are determined largely by your irrational Beliefs, the next step is to identify these Beliefs as they existed in the episode under consideration. As part of this identification exercise, it is important that you distinguish these irrational Beliefs from their rational alternatives. This task is fairly straightforward if you bear in mind the points I made in Chapter 3. If you recall, in that chapter I pointed out that there are four major irrational Beliefs:

(i)   Unmet demands (or musts);
(ii)   Self-depreciation;
(iii)   Awfulizing; and
(iv)   Low Frustration Tolerance (LFT).

The rational alternatives to these irrational Beliefs are as follows (see Chapter 8 for a review):

(i)   Unmet preferences;
(ii)   Unconditional self-acceptance;
(iii)   Anti-awfulizing; and
(iv)   High Frustration Tolerance (HFT).

Let's see how Marie put this information into practice. First, after she acknowledged that she felt ashamed about revealing a weakness about crying in front of her boss, Marie looked for her 'must' which, she realized, lay at the core of her shame. She showed herself that she did not just prefer not showing her boss her weakness. She demanded that she must not do so.

Second, Marie looked for her self-depreciating Belief. She accepted that she was not only evaluating her presumed weakness as bad, but that she was putting herself down as a weak, defective person for having that weakness.

Third, Marie looked for her awfulizing Belief. She appreciated that when she felt ashamed she was not just saying that it was bad that she revealed a weakness to her boss. She acknowledged that she was making a grossly exaggerated awfulizing statement ('It is awful that I revealed a weakness in front of my boss by crying').

Finally, Marie searched for and found her LFT Belief. She accepted that when she felt ashamed she was not just saying that revealing a weakness was difficult to bear. She was telling herself: 'I can't stand it that I revealed a weakness by crying in front of my boss.'

Use what Marie did as a model for identifying your own irrational Beliefs.

Step 8: Challenge these irrational Beliefs by showing yourself that they are false, illogical and self-defeating

Now that you have identified the specific irrational Beliefs that underpin your feelings of shame, the next step is to question these beliefs. The purpose of such questioning is to weaken your conviction in these Beliefs and to work towards feeling healthily disappointed instead. Let me demonstrate how you can question your irrational Beliefs by showing you how Marie challenged hers. She asked herself and answered the following three questions:

(i)   Is my irrational Belief true? (In other words, is it consistent with reality?)

(ii)   Is my irrational Belief sensible or logical?

(iii)   Does my irrational Belief give me healthy results?

As I pointed out in Chapter 3, unmet demands and self-depreciation Beliefs are frequently more central in shame than awfulizing and LFT Beliefs. Consequently, I will focus on Marie's unmet demands and self-depreciating Beliefs in showing you how to answer the above three questions. You can, of course, use the same three questions to challenge your awfulizing and LFT Beliefs.

Let's first take Marie's unmet demand: 'I absolutely should not have revealed a weakness by crying in front of my boss.'

Question: Is this Belief true?
Answer: No. If there was a law of the universe which states that I (Marie) must not show this weakness in front of my boss, then obviously I couldn't go against this law. Try as I might I would not be able to cry in front of him even if I wanted to, I am obviously not immune from revealing this weakness to my boss, thus this Belief is patently false.

Question: Is this Belief sensible?
Answer: No. I certainly prefer not showing a weakness in front of my boss but it makes no sense for me to conclude therefore that I must not show such a weakness. My preference is flexible since it allows for the fact that I did reveal such a weakness and that I wish I hadn't. It is no way logically connected to my demand which is rigid and rules out the possibility of showing a weakness. Rigidity is very different from flexibility and there is no sensible connection between the two.

Question: Does this Belief provide me with healthy results?
Answer: Again the answer to this question is, 'No'. As long as I believe that I must not reveal a weakness by crying in front of my boss, then I will feel ashamed when I do so and anxious in case I do so. My feelings of shame will then lead me to avoid my boss and prevent me from changing this irrational Belief. This Belief will there-fore remain intact and consequently, I will remain vulnerable to shame and anxiety about revealing

another weakness in front of my boss. Thus, this irrational Belief will largely give me poor emotional and behavioural results.

Now let's see how Marie challenged her self-depreciation Belief which was: 'If I show a weakness to my boss by crying in front of him, then I am a weak, defective person.'

Question: Is this Belief true?

Answer: No. It may be true that I have revealed a weakness, but this doesn't make me a weak, defective person. To be weak and defective through and through, everything about me would have to be weak and defective, now, in the past and in the future. This is obviously untrue.

Question: Is this Belief sensible?

Answer: No. When I say that I am a weak and defective person for revealing a weakness, I am committing the part-whole error. In this error, I falsely state that my entire self can be sensibly defined by a part of myself (i.e. my revealing a weakness to my boss). This is obviously an illogical overgeneralization. The whole of something, when it is complex, cannot be defined by one (or more) of its parts.

Question: Does this Belief provide me with healthy results?

Answer: Again the response is 'No'. As long as I believe that I am a weak, defective person for revealing a weakness in front of my boss then once again I will feel ashamed when I do so and anxious in case I do so. My view that I am a weak, defective person for crying in front of my boss will lead me to avoid him whenever possible and prevent me from challenging my irrational Belief. Failing to challenge and change this self-depreciating Belief will render me vulnerable to shame and anxiety as a result. Thus, once again this irrational Belief will largely give me poor emotional and behavioural results.

Using the same three questions, why don't you challenge your own unmet demands and self-depreciation Beliefs as well as your awfulizing and Low Frustration Tolerance Beliefs.

Step 9: Show yourself that the rational alternatives to these irrational Beliefs, by contrast, are true, sensible and yield healthy results

When you challenge your irrational Beliefs, it is like uprooting weeds in a garden. However, if you want your garden to look nice, you then have to plant seeds so that flowers will grow. Thus, if you want your rational Beliefs to grow, you have to plant them into your Belief system. The first step in this process is to apply the same questions to your rational Beliefs as you applied to your irrational Beliefs in the previous step. Doing this enables you to see clearly why your rational Beliefs are rational and helps you to commit yourself to strengthening your conviction in them and to feeling disappointment instead of shame.

In showing you how this can be done, let's see how Marie questioned her rational Beliefs. Let's first take her unmet preference which is: 'I wish that I hadn't revealed a weakness by crying in front of my boss, but there is no reason why I absolutely shouldn't have done so.'

Question: Is this Belief true?

Answer: Yes, this Belief is true. My preference reflects the reality of what I wanted to happen. However, by saying that it didn't have to happen I am acknowledging the reality of what actually happened, i.e. I did reveal a weakness in front of my boss. In general, preferences are a true reflection of what I want to happen, while demands are against reality because it is always possible for my demands not to be met.

Question: Is this Belief sensible?

Answer: Yes, it is sensible. When I hold a specific unmet preference like not wanting to reveal a weakness by crying in front of my boss (but without insisting that I must not do so), this specific preference follows logically from my general philosophy that I desire what I want, but I do not have to get it. This general philosophy is eminently sensible. However, when I believe that I must not reveal such a weakness in front of my boss, this Belief is not sensible because it is not logically connected to my healthy desire.

Question: Does this Belief provide me with healthy results?

Answer: Yes. As long as I believe that I prefer not to reveal a weakness by crying in front of my boss, but I allow for the possibility that I might do so, then I will feel disappointed but not ashamed if I do actually cry in front of him, and concerned but not anxious about the prospect of so doing. My feelings of disappointment will then discourage me from avoiding my boss and will allow me then to focus on and address the factors that led me to cry in the first place. Thus, my rational Belief will largely give me healthy emotional and behavioural results in the face of a negative activating event like crying in front of my boss which I infer is a weakness.

Now let me show you how Marie questioned her self-acceptance Belief, namely: 'If I cry in front of my boss and thus reveal a weakness to him, this does not make me a weak, defective person. Rather I am a fallible human being who on this occasion acted weakly.'

Question: Is this Belief true?

Answer: Yes. I can prove that I am a fallible human being who has the capability to act strongly and weakly for that is the essence of being human. I can also disprove that I am a weak and defective person, for if this were true everything about me would be weak and defective and I would be incapable of acting strongly. All of which is patently false.

89

Question: Is this Belief sensible?

Answer: Yes. When I conclude that I am a fallible human being, with strengths and weaknesses, for revealing a weakness in front of my boss, such a conclusion is logical since my specific revealed weakness does not mean that I have no strengths. Thus, I am not making the part-whole error discussed on p. 87. When I conclude that revealing a weakness to my boss makes me a weak, defective person, I rule out the possibility that I have any strengths, a conclusion which is not sensible.

Question: Does this Belief provide me with healthy results?

Answer: Once again the answer to this question is, 'Yes'. As long as I believe that revealing a weakness in front of my boss proves that I am fallible, I will be disappointed, but not ashamed about doing so. I will thus have no reason to avoid him or others who may learn of the incident. This Belief will also help me to reflect on why I cried in the first place, which my shame-creating irrational Belief will not help me to do. My self-acceptance Belief and the feelings of disappointment which result will encourage me to gain the understanding I need to work towards dealing with my boss's criticism without tears if I finally decide that this is my goal. Thus, once again, this rational, self-acceptance Belief will give me healthy emotional and behavioural results.

Using Marie's answers as a guide, why don't you now apply the three questions to your rational unmet preference and self-acceptance Beliefs. You can also apply the same questions to your anti-awfulizing and High Frustration Tolerance Beliefs.

Step 10: Act on your new rational Belief

One of the best ways of integrating your new rational Belief into your Belief system is to act on this Belief. You need to select those actions that would be consistent with your new rational Belief. Also, after you have chosen these actions it is important to realize that you need to put them into practice repeatedly if you are going to internalize your new rational Belief.

As you draw up your action plan, you may find two points particularly helpful. First, you may find it useful to act on a concept that I have called 'challenging, but not overwhelming' when planning your behavioural homework. By this I mean doing something that you would find challenging, but which you would not find overwhelming at that time. Some people find it helpful to draw up a hierarchy of tasks from minimally challenging to maximally challenging. Second, it is important for you to delib-erately rehearse your new rational Belief before you carry out your behavioural task and while you are carrying it out.

I put these two ideas into practice while overcoming my shame about stammering when I was about seventeen. In my childhood and adolescence, I had a very bad stammer about which I was very ashamed. My shame led me either to avoid speaking whenever I thought I would stammer or to use various tricks, the purpose of which was to help me avoid using words beginning with 'd', 'b', 'c', 'k' or 'p' and followed by a vowel – words which I found particularly difficult to pronounce without stammering. I realized that my shame was based on two irrational Beliefs: (i) 'I must not stammer in public and if I do this would prove that I am defective'; and (ii) 'If I stammer, people will laugh at me which they must not do. If they laugh at me, this will prove once again that I am defective.'

First, I questioned these irrational Beliefs and developed the following rational alternatives: (i) 'I would much prefer it if I did not stammer in public, but there is no reason why I must not do so. If I stammer in public this would only prove that I am a fallible human being with a speech defect. I would not be a defective person'; and (ii) 'There is no reason why people must not laugh at me if I stammer, although I would much prefer it if they didn't. But if they do, I can once again accept myself as a person with a speech defect. If they think I'm a defective person, they're wrong.'

Second, armed with these two Beliefs, I resolved to speak up as often as possible while not avoiding using words which I found difficult to pronounce. Initially, I would go into shops and ask to purchase cheap items whether I needed them or not. Then, I resolved to speak on the phone as often as I could – previously, I avoided using the phone. Then, I went to meetings and spoke up at every opportunity, something that I would not have done previously. Every time I spoke up I would rehearse whichever new rational Belief was most applicable overtly before I spoke and covertly while in the act of speaking. I also stopped trying not to stammer because I discovered that if I tried not to stammer, I stammered more!

About a year later, a number of things had happened. First, I had conquered my shame about stammering although I felt disappointed when I did so; second, I stammered far less than hitherto; and third, I realized that very few people laughed at me and on the odd occasion when they did, I did not feel ashamed. Rather, I felt irritated about their immaturity. Now, I can speak on national radio or television without a hint of shame when I stammer and sometimes relate this story on the media to help other people who stammer. Note that I have just used the phrase 'people who stammer'. I do so advisedly for I also discovered that when I thought of myself as a stammerer, it hindered my attempts to overcome my shame and conversely, when I realized that I was not a stammerer, but a person who stammered some of the time and spoke fluently at other times, this more accurate idea helped me to overcome my shame problem.

Returning to the case of Marie, in order to practise acting in accord with her new rational Belief she sought out her boss and asked him to tell her when he was unhappy with her work, even pushing him to be critical. When he did so she could feel tears welling up inside her, but rehearsed her rational Belief (that she was not a weak, defective person, but was a fallible human being if she openly cried in front of him) while meeting his gaze. She also asked her colleagues whether they had heard about the incident when she cried in front of her boss and asked them what they thought of her for shedding tears. Again she did this while rehearsing the rational Belief that she could accept herself as a fallible human being even if they were critical of her for crying. She also made every effort to take part in social events with her colleagues and resisted her remaining action tendency to avoid their company. These behavioural tasks helped Marie to internalize her new rational Beliefs.

Step 11: Question your shame-derived thinking

In Chapters 5 and 6, I discussed how shame can lead you to make further distorted inferences about elements of the situation about which you feel ashamed. At this point, it is important that you stand back and consider the likely truth of these inferences. Feeling disappointed but not ashamed will help you to be objective about your previously distorted inferences.

In Marie's case, her feelings of disappointment led her to think that while her boss might look down on her for crying, this was unlikely given what she knew about him. She appreciated that while he might tell everyone in the office, this was very unlikely. Furthermore, she reasoned that even if he did tell everyone in the office about her 'weakness', most of her colleagues would not look down on her or pity her. She also concluded that those who learned about the incident would soon forget about it. She tested out these more realistic inferences by asking her boss for critical feedback and by asking her colleagues for their opinions about her for crying in front of her boss. These actions confirmed the truth of her new, more realistic inferences.

When you come to challenge your shame-derived inferences, here are some useful questions to ask yourself:

(i)   How realistic is my thinking here?
(ii)   How else can I view this situation?
(iii)   How likely is it that my inference is true?
(iv)   Would twelve objective judges agree that my inference is correct?
(v)   What inference would these twelve objective judges make instead?
(vi)   If I told someone, whom I could trust to give me an objective opinion about the truth or falsity of my inference, what would this person say to me?

(vii) If someone told me that they had made this inference about the same situation, what would I say to this person about the validity of their inference?

(viii) What data do I need to gather to check the validity of my inference and how reliable will such data be?

Step 12: Reconsider the inference that you made at **A**

You will recall that in Step 5 I asked you to identify what you felt most ashamed about in the incident that you chose to analyse. I also urged you to assume temporarily that this inference was true. I encouraged you to do this to help you to identify the irrational Beliefs that lay at the core of your feelings of shame. If you had changed your inference at this point in the change sequence you might have stopped feeling ashamed, but you would have achieved this without identifying, challenging and changing the irrational Beliefs that really determined your feelings of shame. If you had bypassed your irrational Beliefs at this point you would still be vulnerable to feeling ashamed about the event in question if you later returned to your previous inference. In addition, if you had challenged your major inference about **A** without first going on to challenge your irrational Beliefs, your view would have been coloured by the ongoing existence of these irrational Beliefs.

You are in a much better position, therefore, to question your inference about **A** when you have challenged and changed your irrational Beliefs. Doing so will help you to be objective in your judgements about the inference you made about **A**. Putting this differently, feeling disappointed will help you to stand back and take an objective view about your inference, while feeling ashamed will interfere with your objectivity. When you come to evaluate your inference about **A**, why not ask yourself the eight questions that I detailed above on pp. 93–4.

Feeling disappointed but not ashamed about revealing a weakness by crying in front of her boss, helped Marie to be objective about her major inference that crying in front of her boss constituted a weakness. On thinking about this issue, but this time from a more objective position, Marie concluded (with the help of similar questions that I detailed on pp. 93–4) that while it was an unpleasant experience, shedding tears was not a weakness. Rather, it was an unfortunate expression of her upsetness about being unfairly criticized.

I have now outlined the twelve steps that you need to take to overcome your feelings of situational shame. In the next chapter, I will offer some advice about what you need to do in order to become less shame-prone.

11

How to become less shame-prone

In Chapter 6, I distinguished between situational shame and shame-proneness. If you are experiencing situational shame, you are feeling ashamed in a specific situation. If you are highly prone to shame, you will experience shame in many different situations that you cannot avoid and you will avoid other situations in which you would otherwise experience shame.

I further distinguish between low shame-proneness (LSP) and high shame-proneness (HSP). If you have LSP, you will experience situational shame in a small number of situations and you will not tend to develop a general pattern of avoidance, while if you have HSP, as I said above, you will experience situational shame in many different situations and you will tend to develop a general pattern of avoidance.

In this chapter, I will discuss steps that you need to take if you are highly prone to shame. Before I do so, let me state that if you have HSP, there may well be limits to what you can achieve from a self-help book such as this. You may well need and benefit from an extended period of counselling. This does not mean that you are sick or mentally ill. Far from it. It just means that because you are prone to shame, your life is quite painful and severely restricted. You may have few friends and may avoid situations where you can develop acquaintances and friendships. You may be very shy, be deficient in social skills and think that nobody would be interested in you. If you do make friends, you may well live in fear that you will be found out as a fraud and that when people really get to know you they will discover what an insignificant, worthless or defective person you really are.

If you recognize yourself in this description, I hope that you will see that you are not sick or mentally ill, but are a person who is in a lot of psychological pain and who needs professional help. It is not shameful to seek counselling; thousands upon thousands of people do. With skilled counselling over an extended period of time, you

96

will make much progress if you are prepared to put into practice what you learn from counselling. This is exactly what happened to Sarah who I first discussed in Chapter 1 (see Chapter 12 for a discussion of what Sarah, who was highly prone to shame, achieved from counselling). If you want to see a counsellor, discuss this in the first instance with your GP.

Having said all this, what if you want to become less shame-prone, but do not wish or are unable to seek counselling? What follows is a brief discussion of the steps that you need to take.

Step 1: Identify the situations that you feel ashamed about

The first step that you need to take is to make a comprehensive list of what you feel ashamed about. When you make this list, include both situations in which you have felt ashamed and situations that you have avoided for fear of feeling ashamed if you had encountered them.

Step 2: Identify common inference themes

The second step is to look through all these situations and identify common inference themes, assuming once again temporarily that they are true. An example of a common inference theme would be 'revealing a weakness in social situations', if this is what you feel ashamed about in a significant number of the situations you have listed. At this point you might find it helpful to reread Chapter 2 where I discuss what people tend to feel ashamed about, before you identify your common inference themes.

Step 3: Identify your general, shame-related, irrational Beliefs

The next step is to identify your general, shame-related, irrational Beliefs. Thus, if one of your common inference themes is 'revealing a weakness in social situations', your general, irrational Beliefs would be:

(i)   I must not reveal a weakness in social situations.
(ii)   If I reveal a weakness in social situations, this will prove that I
       am a weak person.
(iii) It is terrible if I reveal a weakness in social situations.
(iv)   I cannot bear it if I reveal a weakness in social situations.

Identify your general, shame-related, irrational Beliefs for every
common inference theme you have identified.

Step 4: Challenge your general irrational Beliefs

In this step you need to challenge your general irrational Beliefs
using the three questions that I discussed in the previous chapter, i.e.

(i)   Is this Belief true?
(ii)   Is this Belief sensible?
(iii) Does this Belief give me healthy emotional and behavioural
       results?

Reread the previous chapter for guidance on how to answer these
questions.

Step 5: Develop general rational alternatives to your general irrational Beliefs

In this step, you need to develop general rational alternatives to your
irrational Beliefs for each of the common inference themes that you
have identified. If one of your common inference themes is
'revealing a weakness in social situations', your general rational
Beliefs would be:

(i)   I would prefer it if I did not reveal a weakness in social
       situations, but there is no reason why I must not do so.
(ii)   If I reveal a weakness in social situations, this would not prove
       that I am a weak person. It would prove that I am a fallible

human being who can reveal both strengths and weaknesses in public.

(iii) It is bad if I reveal a weakness in social situations, but it is not terrible.

(iv) I can bear it if I reveal a weakness in social situations, although I do not like doing so.

Then, you need to question these general rational Beliefs in the same way as you questioned your general irrational Beliefs (see Chapter 10 for guidance on this point).

Step 6: Identify the strategies you employ to avoid or get rid of shame

In this sixth step, you need to identify and list the strategies that you employ either to prevent feeling ashamed or to get rid of shame as soon as you experience it. Reread Chapters 4 and 5 for a list of these strategies. Ensure that you have listed such strategies for each common inference theme.

Step 7: Develop healthy alternatives to these strategies based on your general rational Beliefs and resolve to put these new strategies into practice

The strategies that you use to avoid or get rid of shame are based on the existence of your general, shame-related, irrational Beliefs. Since you have now developed a set of disappointment-related rational Beliefs, you will not need to use these strategies. However, if you do not develop and resolve to put into practice a healthy set of alternative strategies, you may still be tempted to employ your shame-avoidant and shame-eradicating strategies because they are well-ingrained and you have nothing else to put into their place.

Thus, in this step you need to develop a set of strategies based on your new rational Beliefs. Choose an alternative healthy strategy for each shame-avoidant and shame-eradicating strategy that you listed in the previous step. See Chapter 9 for a discussion of such strategies.

Step 8: Identify your shame-influenced action and thinking tendencies

In Step 6, I asked you to identify strategies that you employ to prevent shame or to get rid of this emotion before you have fully experienced it. In this step, your task is different. Here, you need to think about how you tend to act and think *after* you have experienced shame. List such shame-based action and thinking tendencies for each common inference theme (see Chapters 4, 5 and 6).

Step 9: Develop a list of alternative healthy action and thinking tendencies based on your general disappointment-related, rational Beliefs

In Step 5, you developed a list of general rational Beliefs which would lead you to experience disappointment in relation to your common inference themes. In this step you need to develop a list of action and thinking tendencies that stem from disappointment (see Chapter 9 for a list of such tendencies). Make sure that for every shame-based action and thinking tendency you have listed an alternative tendency, based this time on the feeling of disappointment. Do this for each common inference theme.

Step 10: Act on your general rational Beliefs while rehearsing them

This step is perhaps the most important step of all. For unless you act on your general rational Beliefs you will not internalize them. There are a number of sub-steps to follow here:

(i)   Take one common inference theme at a time.

(ii)   Once you have decided on a particular common inference
        theme, develop a list of situations that reflect this theme and
        list them in order of difficulty.

(iii)   Confront each situation, working your way up the hierarchy,
        from the least difficult to the most difficult. For example, if
        we take the common inference theme 'revealing a weakness
        in social situations', your least difficult situation might be:
        'Going out with a close friend where I might reveal a mild
        weakness', and your most difficult situation might be:
        'Attending a formal dinner where I don't know the protocol of
        the situation and where I might reveal a serious weakness'.

(iv)   As you confront each situation, make sure that you rehearse
        your rational Belief (specific or general).

(v)   Guard against putting into practice any shame-related strat-
        egy (listed in Steps 6 and 8 above). Instead use the alternative
        strategies listed in Steps 7 and 9 above.

(vi)   Repeat sub-steps ii–v for every common inference theme.

Step 11: Carry out deliberate shame-attacking exercises

In the previous step, I encouraged you to act on your general rational
Beliefs by confronting situations where you *may* encounter actual
examples of your common inference theme (e.g. revealing a
weakness in social situations). While doing so will give you
valuable practice at acting on these rational Beliefs, you may well
not encounter examples of your common inference pattern, i.e. you
may well not actually reveal a weakness in a particular social
situation. In Step 11, you undertake deliberately to bring about your
common inference theme (e.g. you set out deliberately to reveal a
weakness in a social situation while rehearsing at the same time
your rational Belief). This is known as carrying out shame-
attacking exercises.

    If you are going to undertake such exercises, a word of caution.
Do not do anything that is illegal, immoral, likely to unduly alarm
others or jeopardize your job or your friendships. If you follow

these guidelines, then carrying out shame-attacking exercises can be a powerful way of internalizing your general rational Beliefs.

Step 12: Reconsider your specific inferences and develop new common inference themes

In the previous chapter on situational shame, I suggested that you reconsider the adequacy of your inference at **A** after you have developed and acted on your specific rational Belief. The same is true with respect to becoming less shame-prone. So at this step, based on your general rational Belief, stand back and reconsider each inference at **A** that comprises your common inference theme. Once you have reconsidered these inferences, develop a new common inference theme which best describes these reconsidered inferences. Do this for each shame-related common inference theme. Use this new common inference theme when you are tempted to make specific shame-related inferences.

These, then, are the steps that you need to take if you are to become less shame-prone. However, we are not quite finished, for there are two points that you need to remember if you are to sustain your progress.

Point 1: Becoming less shame-prone takes repeated practice

If you are highly prone to shame, you will probably be very sceptical if someone tells you that it doesn't take much practice to become less shame-prone. You would be correct to be sceptical. For becoming less prone to shame does, unfortunately, take much repeated practice along the lines that I have discussed in this chapter. However, if you are willing to commit yourself to carrying out such practice, you will in all probability become less shame-prone. As I pointed out at the beginning of this chapter, you may need the help of a counsellor during this process, but if you are working on your own and you follow the above guidelines, then you will still make progress.

Point 2: *The path to becoming less shame-prone is rarely smooth*

Like any personal change project, the path to becoming less shame-prone will rarely be smooth. Sometimes you may take two steps forward and one step back, and at other times you may take one step forward and two back. This is normal and you should expect this. While you will experience the occasional lapse in your progress, you need to learn from this lapse and not disturb yourself about it. Not learning from a lapse and disturbing yourself about it are two ways in which you can convert a lapse into a relapse.

Thus, when you experience a lapse in your progress, it is important that you identify the factors involved so you can address and overcome them. For example, you may find yourself returning to old, dysfunctional, shame-preventing or shame-eradicating strategies. If so, this probably means that you are returning to your old, shame-creating, irrational Beliefs; in which case, you need to identify, challenge and change these Beliefs as described in Steps 3 to 5 above. Indeed, you may find it useful to use the above twelve steps as a framework for identifying and dealing with factors associated with lapses.

Two other factors associated with lapses are worth highlighting because they are quite common. The first involves you feeling ashamed about your feelings of shame. I discussed how to handle this issue in the previous chapter (see pp. 81–2) and it is worth reviewing this material if you think it applies to you. The second factor associated with lapses is found when you hold a philosophy of Low Frustration Tolerance (LFT) about the change process itself. Thus, you may think that working to become less shame-prone is *too* hard or *too* boring. If this is the case, then it is important to challenge these irrational Beliefs. Show yourself that the change process may well be hard or boring, but this hardly means that it is *too* hard or *too* boring.

If it is hard, then show yourself that (i) it is worth doing this hard work in order to gain the benefits from such work; (ii) it is harder for you in the long term if you don't do this work; and (iii) the work may well be hard, but it will become easier the more you do it. If you find the work boring, then show yourself again that it is worth doing this boring work in order to profit from it and then find ways of improvising so that the work is less boring.

If you think that you have a particular problem in dealing with LFT, then you might benefit from reading a book I wrote with Jack Gordon entitled *Beating the Comfort Trap* (Sheldon Press, 1993) and from implementing the ideas contained therein.

Before I bring this chapter to a close, let me remind you that if you are prone to shame, you still experience this emotion in specific situations and therefore you will gain benefit from reading the previous chapter and implementing the step-by-step guide to overcoming situational shame.

In the last chapter, I will return to the cases I first introduced in Chapter 1 and show how they could and in some cases did overcome shame.

12

From shame to disappointment: the case examples revisited

In this final chapter, I will return to the case examples I first presented in Chapter 1 and show what the people concerned would have had to have done (and in some cases actually did) to feel disappointment rather than shame.

Marie

You will no doubt remember the case of Marie, as I have used her to illustrate many of the points that I have made throughout this book. You will therefore recall that Marie felt ashamed about crying in front of her boss in response to his criticism of her. Her shame was partly related to the inference she made that her crying was a weakness, but was more centrally determined by the irrational Belief she held about this event. This was primarily: 'I must not reveal a weakness by crying in front of my boss. The fact that I have done so proves that I am a weak, defective person.'

Holding this Belief, Marie could not look her boss in the eye and experienced an overwhelming impulse to run out of the room, which she did. Later, her feelings of shame led her to think that her boss would look down on her for crying, that he would tell everyone in the office who would then either look down on her or pity her. She thought that everyone would hear about this incident and would remember it forever. She resolved there and then to avoid her boss as much as possible and certainly when she was upset, and concluded from that moment to keep herself to herself when it came to dealing with her work colleagues.

I discussed, in Chapter 10, how Marie could have challenged the two parts of this irrational Belief by showing herself that they were inconsistent with reality, illogical, and detrimental to her well-being. Instead, she could have constructed the following rational Belief: 'I would have much preferred not to have publicly revealed a weakness by crying in front of my boss, but there is no reason why I absolutely should not have done so. I am a fallible human being for revealing such a weakness. I am not a weak, defective person.'

Holding this new rational Belief, Marie would have felt disappointed rather than ashamed about crying in front of her boss and would have been able to stay in the room, look her boss in the eye and tell him that she thought he was unfair in his criticism. Later, her feelings of disappointment would have led her to think that while her boss might look down on her for crying, this was unlikely given what she knew about him. She would have appreciated that while he might tell everyone in the office, this was very unlikely. Furthermore, she would have reasoned that even if he did tell everyone in the office about her 'weakness', most of her colleagues would not look down on her or pity her. She would have concluded also that those who learned about the incident would soon forget about it. Subsequently, she would not have avoided her boss even when she was upset, and she would have mixed with her colleagues as much as she did prior to this incident. Finally, on thinking about whether or not crying in front of her boss was a weakness, she may well have concluded that while it was an unpleasant experience, shedding tears was not a weakness. Rather, it was an unfortunate expression of her upsetness about being unfairly criticized.

Elise

Elise was one of my clients and has given me permission to tell her story and how she responded to therapy. If you recall from Chapter 1, Elise was a young Orthodox Jewish woman who had grown up without any sexual education. She recognized at quite an early age that she had strong sexual feelings, but she had no outlet to express them. One night she had an erotic dream where she was caressing and was being caressed by another woman and she felt deeply ashamed about this and the fact that she experienced an orgasm during this dream. Knowing very little about female sexuality and feeling deeply ashamed about the sexual feelings that she experienced during the dream, Elise concluded that she must be a lesbian, a realization that she found horrific. She then tried to avoid looking at women and tried to keep her physical distance from them. This only made things worse and she found herself unwittingly looking at the breasts and crotches of other women in the street.

On realizing that she was becoming more and more aware of other women as sexual beings, she became increasingly ashamed and resolved to avoid all situations where women might be. Since she was a college student and had to study with other women, her increasing feelings of shame led her to think that her fellow students (especially the female students) would know that she was a lesbian and that people in her religious community would find out with the result that she would become an outcast. Furthermore, she was convinced she would never marry and have children. She came to see me for counselling specifically because I was a man and when I first saw her she was quite suicidal.

I first explained the A–B–C model of emotion to Elise and showed her that even if she was a lesbian (which of course was the inference that she drew from the dream that she had), this 'fact' did not cause her shame. Rather, it was her irrational Beliefs at **B** about this presumed 'fact' at **A** that best explained her feelings of shame at **C**. I also explained that our first task in therapy was to have her assume temporarily that she was a lesbian, so that we could examine her irrational Beliefs and change them to their rational alternatives. This would lead her to feel disappointed but not ashamed about being a lesbian, which would in turn help her to calm down and examine objectively the evidence for and against her being a lesbian.

Initially, Elise was doubtful about this strategy because she wanted to be reassured that she was not a lesbian. I explained that even if I reassured her at this point that she was not a lesbian, her irrational Beliefs and the shame that stemmed from these Beliefs meant that she was not reassurable on this issue. This made sense to Elise and we proceeded to identify and challenge the following irrational Beliefs: 'I must, under no circumstances, be a lesbian. If I am this would prove that I am a thoroughly shameful person and would be shunned by my community. If this happened, it would be terrible and I would not be able to tolerate it.' These Beliefs explained why Elise was suicidal and accounted for her widespread avoidance of other women.

Our counselling work helped Elise thoroughly to challenge these Beliefs and to develop the following rational alternatives:

> I would much prefer not to be a lesbian, but there is no law of the universe to decree that I, or any other woman, must not have this sexual orientation. If I am a lesbian, I am one; and while I would find this difficult to come to terms with because of my upbringing, it would not be unbearable. Without minimizing what being a lesbian would mean for my life as an Orthodox Jew, there are far worse things in life and it is certainly not terrible. If I were a lesbian, I certainly wouldn't like it, but I would not be a shameful person. I would still be an unrateable, unique, fallible human being who does not like one important part of myself. I do not have to dislike and shun my whole self even if, as is likely, my Orthodox religious community will shun me.

Armed with this set of rational Beliefs, Elise sought out the company of women. This helped her to calm down and she stopped being obsessed with the genitals or breasts of other women. Because she was now very disappointed but not ashamed about the prospect of being a lesbian, she was ready to receive some sexual education and I suggested that she read a book on female sexuality. Her feelings of disappointment and this new knowledge helped her to stand back and consider the evidence for and against being a lesbian. On examining her waking sexual fantasies and her sexual feelings, she concluded that she was basically heterosexual, but that she, like numerous other women, did have some mild sexual feelings towards a small handful of other women. Her dogmatic insistence that she be 100 per cent heterosexual meant that she labelled her 'lesbian' feelings as forbidden – a process which increased their intensity.

After our counselling finished, she lost her virginity to a man that she had begun to date and years later she is still going out with him. She is comfortable with her sexuality and no longer feels ashamed of any sexual feelings she experiences towards other women.

Rick

Rick, if you recall, was a leading member of a local street gang whose code of honour was that whatever happened gang members stuck together and would never betray one another. This code was violated by Geoff, a gang member who 'grassed' on Freddy who stabbed a rival gang member during a fight. Rick was ashamed about Geoff's behaviour partly because Geoff had broken the gang's code of honour and according to Rick had shown the gang in a very bad light in the local community, but primarily because of Rick's irrational Belief that Geoff must not betray the gang and because he did, this proved that Rick and the other gang members were diminished as humans. Rick's feelings of shame led him to keep a very low profile in the community, avoiding all places where other gang members might be found. His shame also led him to think that as a result of Geoff's behaviour, other people in the community would hold Rick and his gang in contempt in that they had 'gone soft' and were no longer a force to be reckoned with in 'gangland'.

In order for Rick to have felt disappointed but not ashamed about Geoff's betrayal of the gang he would have had to challenge his irrational Belief using the three questions discussed in Chapter 10, i.e. 'Is it true?', 'Is it sensible?' and 'Is it conducive to my psychological well-being?' After proving to himself that the answer to these questions was 'No', Rick would have developed the following alternative rational Belief: 'It would have been highly desirable if Geoff had not betrayed the gang, but there is no reason why he must not have done so. I and the other gang members are not diminished as humans by Geoff's behaviour, even if other people may think so. Our worth cannot be defined by the behaviour of another gang member.'

Because he would have felt disappointed rather than ashamed,

Rick would have been able to carry on as normal and would not have kept a low profile in the community. His new feelings of disappointment would have led him to acknowledge that while some people in the community might hold Rick and his gang in contempt, others would not do so. He would have thus been able to take a realistic view of the consequences of the betrayal.

Tom

I also introduced Tom in Chapter 1. Tom was a short young man who was deeply ashamed of his height. To compensate, Tom would seize on every opportunity to show other people (and, of course, himself) how macho he was. To help him do this he studied martial arts and pumped iron. He would deliberately pick fights with taller guys, taking great satisfaction from beating them up. He would revel in picking up and seducing women taller than himself. 'Love 'em and leave 'em' was Tom's motto.

If you recall, Tom was badly beaten in a fight and he felt very ashamed of this. To get away from his shame, Tom moved to a different part of the country and vowed never to return to his home town, convinced as he was that people would still remember the day when he was revealed in his true, 'wimp' colours.

Tom's shame about his beating was based on his demand: 'I must never be beaten in a fight and have my "wimpness" revealed. Because this happened, it proves that I am a wimp, a laughing stock for all to see.' If Tom had been helped to challenge this irrational Belief, he could have developed the following rational Belief: 'I wish I wasn't beaten in that fight and had not had my "wimpness" revealed, but there is no reason why I have to be invincible. I am not a wimp, but a fallible human being who has strengths and weaknesses.' If Tom believed this, he would have felt keenly disappointed about his beating, but not ashamed of it. Feeling disappointed but not ashamed, there would have been no need for him to leave the neighbourhood since he would have then realized that he was not a laughing stock in most people's eyes.

Tom would have then been motivated to question his more general irrational Beliefs: 'My short stature is a sign that I am less manly than I must be. This means that I am a wimp. I cannot bear this and I must take every step to cover up and compensate for my true identity.' In doing this he would have first assumed temporarily that his shortness was a sign of unmanliness and then proved to himself that: 'There is no law of the universe which states that I have to be as manly as I want to be, although it is quite healthy to want this.'

Being unmanly in one respect does not prove that my true identity is that of a wimp. Rather my true identity is that of a fallible human being with strengths and weaknesses (one of which is my short stature). I can bear my short stature even though I may never like it, and since I am not a wimp, there is no need to compensate for this or cover it up.

This rational Belief would have helped Tom to be disappointed about his short stature rather than deeply ashamed of it. He would then have given up trying to prove to everyone, including himself, how macho he was. He would thus have developed healthier relationships with both men and women and lived a far less violent lifestyle.

Bernice

If you remember from Chapter 1, Bernice had been sexually abused by an uncle when she was eight. She was ashamed that she let her uncle abuse her without putting up a struggle and she was ashamed about her body, believing even in adulthood that her body would reveal her shameful secret. Bernice felt this way because of the following irrational Beliefs: (i) 'I absolutely should have tried to stop my uncle from abusing me and the fact that I didn't proves that I am a weak, pathetic person'; and (ii) 'I am a disgusting person for having been abused and my body shows my disgustingness. Thus, nobody must see my body.'

You will recall that as a consequence of her feelings of shame, Bernice had sexual problems and could not let anyone see her naked body. Once her feelings of shame were activated, Bernice thought that if others saw any part of her body: (i) they would see her as a shameful person for having let her uncle abuse her; (ii) they would consider her sexually promiscuous and 'asking for it'; and (iii) they would be revolted by her body. Thus, when she felt ashamed, she would cover herself from head to toe even on hot, summer days to hide her mark of shame.

In order for Bernice to overcome her shame she would have had to challenge her irrational Beliefs and show herself that they are false, illogical and detrimental to her mental health. Doing this would have helped her to develop the following rational Beliefs: (i) 'It would have been much better if I had tried to stop my uncle from abusing me, but there is no law of nature which states that I absolutely should have done. The fact that I did not try to stop him proves that I was a frightened eight-year-old. I am still fallible now and in no way am I a weak, pathetic person; and (ii) I am not a disgusting person for having been abused and therefore my body cannot show my disgustingness. Since I am a fallible person who was treated disgustingly and am not a disgusting person, there is no reason why I cannot show my body when it is appropriate to do so.' If Bernice had resolved to practise these new rational Beliefs while showing her body in suitable circumstances, and if she had resisted her action tendency to cover up her body, then she would have begun to internalize these new rational Beliefs. However, she would still have felt disappointed when she thought about the abuse – a response that would have been very healthy.

Mohammed

Mohammed was the young man who felt ashamed for letting down his family, his religious group and his close-knit Muslim community when he was sent to prison for credit-card fraud in order to fund his expensive spending habits. Mohammed's feelings of shame stemmed from the following irrational Belief: 'I absolutely should not have let down my family, religious group and local Muslim community and because I have done so, I am a defective person and a pariah.'

As a result of his feelings of shame, Mohammed refused to see any visitors in prison and was sorely tempted to give up the Muslim faith. He thought that on release he would be treated as a pariah by his family and community and that no one who knew him would ever forget what he had done. He also had visions of young children pointing him out in the street as some kind of leper.

In prison, Mohammed was helped by a psychologist to take responsibility for his actions and to challenge his shame-creating irrational Belief in the way that I have outlined in this book. As a result, Mohammed was helped to develop and internalize the following rational Belief: 'I really wished that I hadn't let down my family, religious group and local Muslim community, but the reality is that I have done so and unfortunately, there is no universal law that exists which would have prevented me from having done so. I am not a defective person, but a fallible human being with a defect that I resolve to address and overcome. I am not a pariah even though some people may treat me as such.'

As a result of changing his Belief, Mohammed felt deeply disappointed, but not ashamed about his actions and letting down so many people. Doing so helped him to embrace his Muslim faith and to resolve to work on overcoming his spending addiction which he did with the help of the prison psychologist. His deep disappointment helped him to seek the support of local Muslims (which he received) and to think realistically about how others would treat him on his release. Thus, he realized that some people from his community would shun him, but he acknowledged that others would help and support him. His realistic appraisal of this situation turned out to be accurate. A year after his release, even those who shunned him held Mohammed up as a shining example of how embracing the Muslim faith could help people rise above adversity.

Sarah

The last case example that I introduced in Chapter 1 was Sarah, a 33-year-old woman, who suffered from chronic feelings of general shame. For as long as she could remember, Sarah viewed herself as a defective person whom others would find repellent if they got to know her. Sarah held this Belief very strongly and it seemed that nothing could shake it. Not only did this Belief lead Sarah to experience a lot of shame in her life across a broad range of situations where she felt she had to be present; it also meant that Sarah avoided many social situations at which she would have liked to have been present because her presence in these situations would have led her to feel shame.

Because of this avoidance, Sarah failed to acquire the social skills that would enable her, at the very least, to get by socially. Because she lacked these social skills, Sarah was constantly saying inappropriate things in public gatherings when she could not avoid them. She quickly felt ashamed as soon as she became aware of what she had said, which she saw as further evidence that she was defective.

Sarah sought counselling from a Rational Emotive Behaviour Therapist who, over a two-year period, helped her to accept herself as a fallible human being with social difficulties, but who was not a defective person. Sarah's counsellor also taught her social skills which Sarah practised in a number of social situations. Sarah was encouraged to go against her well-ingrained habit of social withdrawal and to resist the temptation of saying inappropriate things in public. When she did say such things, Sarah broke the vicious circle of shame and avoidance by accepting herself as a human being who had just said something inappropriate, but who could remain in the situation and return to the same social setting at the earliest opportunity. At the end of counselling, Sarah had broken a lifelong pattern of shame, social avoidance and loneliness.

You have now reached the end of this book. I hope you found it valuable and I would appreciate hearing about your attempts to put my ideas into practice, c/o Sheldon Press. Have a shame-free life!

Index

Up High 65
Hold Your Head Up High
(Hauck) 65

ideals: disappointment 57–9;
self-rating 66, 68

learning from experience 33–4,
75–6

Maultsby Jr, Maxie C. 67

over-generalization 68–9
Overcoming Anger (Dryden)
47, 54

physical appearance 4–5; body
dysmorphic disorder 11, 32;
concealment 31–2;
disappointment as an
alternative 59

Rational Emotive Behaviour
Therapy (REBT) 1; acting
on rational disbeliefs 90–3;
anti-awfulizing and high
frustration tolerance 69–71;
awfulizing 21–2, 84–5;
frustration 84–5; identifying
and challenging your
irrational beliefs 97–9;
indifference 63; low
frustration tolerance 22–3;
met and unmet demands
17–18, 63–4, 84; met and
unmet preferences 16–17,
63, 64, 84; practice and

progress in overcoming
shame 102–4; shame as
unhealthy and negative 43
reference groups 6–7;
disappointment as an
alternative 59–60;
identification with others
3–4; source of shame 11–12
responsibility denial 31, 40–1,
46

self: acceptance in
disappointment 65–9; belief
in your own shamefulness
38–40; defective 20;
depreciation 18–21, 80,
81–2; diminished 19–20;
self-defeating actions 30,
43–5; socially repellent 20–1
sexuality: abuse 5; fears 2–3;
social repellence 20–1
shame: action tendencies
28–34; becoming less
shame-prone 97–104; case
histories 1–7, 48–50,
105–14; failure to learn from
33–4; falling short of ideals
9–11; identifying and
challenging irrational beliefs
83–90; inferences about
events 8–9, 97, 102;
proneness 51, 96–7;
questioning your thinking
93–5; reference groups
11–12; self-deprecation
18–20; shame-attacking
exercises 101–2; situational